THE LAWYER'S GUIDE TO Microsoft® EXCEL 2007

John C. Tredennick

D1402598

LawPractice Management Section

MARKETING • MANAGEMENT • TECHNOLOGY • FINANCE

Commitment to Quality: The Law Practice Management Section is committed to quality in our publications. Our authors are experienced practitioners in their fields. Prior to publication, the contents of all our books are rigorously reviewed by experts to ensure the highest quality product and presentation. Because we are committed to serving our readers' needs, we welcome your feedback on how we can improve future editions of this book.

Microsoft is a registered trademark of the Microsoft Corporation.

Cover design by Jim Colao.

Nothing contained in this book is to be considered as the rendering of legal advice for specific cases, and readers are responsible for obtaining such advice from their own legal counsel. This book and any forms and agreements herein are intended for educational and informational purposes only.

The products and services mentioned in this publication are under or may be under trademark or service mark protection. Product and service names and terms are used throughout only in an editorial fashion, to the benefit of the product manufacturer or service provider, with no intention of infringement. Use of a product or service name or term in this publication should not be regarded as affecting the validity of any trademark or service mark.

The Law Practice Management Section of the American Bar Association offers an educational program for lawyers in practice. Books and other materials are published in furtherance of that program. Authors and editors of publications may express their own legal interpretations and opinions, which are not necessarily those of either the American Bar Association or the Law Practice Management Section unless adopted pursuant to the bylaws of the Association. The opinions expressed do not reflect in any way a position of the Section or the American Bar Association.

© 2009 American Bar Association. All rights reserved.
Printed in the United States of America.

Library of Congress Cataloging-in-Publication Data
The Lawyer's Guide to Microsoft® Excel 2007. John C. Tredennick:
Library of Congress Cataloging-in-Publication Data is on file.

10-digit: ISBN 1-60442-209-2
13-digit: ISBN 978-1-60442-209-2

12 11 10 09 08   5 4 3 2 1

Discounts are available for books ordered in bulk. Special consideration is given to state bars, CLE programs, and other bar-related organizations. Inquire at Book Publishing, American Bar Association, 321 N. Clark Street, Chicago, Illinois 60654.

Contents

Acknowledgments

Several years ago, my wife told me the next book would be with my next wife. Fortunately, I snuck another one by her. Same wife, new book.

I thank you, Page, for your understanding and indulgence while I goofed around with this project. I thank you Sarah and Scott, my two almost grown children, for all your understanding during the years when Daddy kept working on his laptop and learning something new, while waiting for you to come back from skiing or another birthday party. Sorry for the many Sundays, hidden in the back room when we could have spent more time together. I am doing what I can to make up the time now.

I have several people to thank for the spreadsheets used in the business chapter (which are mostly over my head). My former law partner, Alan Poe, contributed the state tax examples. Minou Bohlin, an accounting and tax guru, shared the income tax example. And my nephew, Steven Tredennick, now a partner at Texas' Bracewell and Giuliani, let me borrow his nifty stock option spreadsheets. I remember when he was just learning algebra. And super-intern Kevin Bell, from C.U. Law School, helped review the manuscript and check the examples (although any errors are mine).

I also have to offer heartfelt thanks to three old friends, Craig Ball, Browning Marean and Joe Kashi (along with Joe's computer-savvy legal assistant, Julie Saltz). Craig reviewed my almost final manuscript with a fine-toothed comb and caught many of the dumb errors that still remained. Browning, Joe and Julie also read it carefully and gave me the ultimate compliment—that I taught them a few tricks that they didn't already know. My thanks to all three for taking the time from their really busy schedules to help make this a better book.

Thank you, too, for choosing this book. I did not do it for the money (of course). Rather, I believe this technology will enrich your practices and even add a little fun in the bargain. My hope is to create a community of spreadsheet-enabled lawyers who can carry the message to the rest of our colleagues.

Trueman, my show-jumping warmblood, also says thanks. He got to laze around the barn while I worked on this. Now that this is done, I can turn off the computer. We are back on the Hunter/Jumper circuit again. Tally Ho.

About the Author

John Tredennick started futzing around with computers in 1988 when his wife moved in with an IBM XT. Since then, he has gotten a bit crazy about it, editing two best-selling books on computers in litigation: W*inning With Computers: Trial Practice in the Twenty-First Century*, Vols. 1 and 2 (American Bar Association, 1991 & 1992); a bunch of articles for different legal magazines; and lecturing all over the world on how lawyers could better use computers. He also wiped out his wife's hard drive (twice) and, generally, made every mistake you could with a computer.

For the first 25 years of his career, Mr. Tredennick was a trial lawyer and partner at Holland & Hart specializing in complex commercial cases. For some of those years, he acted as the firm's Information Technology Partner, directing technology initiatives, and he ran its Trial Partner's Division (now Persuasion Strategies), which offered graphics/multimedia services, jury consulting, litigation support, and web development to firm clients.

In 2000, Mr. Tredennick founded Catalyst Repository Systems, **www.catalystsecure.com**. Catalyst provides web-based repository systems to help distributed teams manage large volumes of documents and work together on complex matters. Its document repositories allow distributed teams to search, review, redact, and produce large volumes of electronic documents. Its collaboration software helps professional teams share files and coordinate efforts on complex cases, claims, and financial transactions. Together, the products provide an integrated platform used by many of the largest organizations in the world for legal, regulatory, and compliance needs.

In his spare time, Mr. Tredennick is active in the ABA too. After editing a litigation-oriented newsletter, he became Articles Editor for *Law Practice Management* magazine and then its Editor for three years. Later, he served as

Chair of the Section and founder and Editor in Chief of its two web-based magazines Webzine, Law Practice Today, **www.lawpracticetoday.org**, and Law Technology Today, **www.lawtechnologytoday.org**.

John and his wife, Page, and children Sarah and Scott ride horses for fun, and all four compete internationally on the show jumping circuit. (Actually, John's horse does most of the work for him.) He and his wife also own a professional cooking school, Cook Street School of Fine Cooking, **www.cookstreet .com**, and a hunter/jumper training barn, **www.woodrunfarm.com**.

John welcomes your visits or correspondence.

Introduction: Why Bother?

For most of my legal career, I did not. I used computers to outline, to word process, to keep track of deadlines, and to organize litigation. But I never saw a need for spreadsheets. Spreadsheets were for accountants. As a litigator, I did not do numbers that often—or at least any I could not handle with ten fingers and a few toes. So, why bother with spreadsheets? Why would I want to learn spreadsheet software?

For me, the answer came several years ago. At the time, I was Articles Editor for *Law Practice Management* magazine, published by the American Bar Association. Each issue included a "Reader Response Card," asking our readers how they liked the issue. The results were tabulated into a simple spreadsheet and sent to me for review.

I could read the survey numbers and make sense of them, but I wanted a better way to display the data for our Editorial Board. For the heck of it, I bought and began learning a $99 spreadsheet program called Quattro Pro. After a couple of plane rides (where I learn most of my computer programs), I was creating color charts and printing them for distribution to the Board. People were amazed at how neat they looked. I was amazed at how simple they were to create.

I had learned charting as a whim, but it soon became handy in my cases. One of my clients was a fast-food franchise with an exclusive lease at a local shopping center. For reasons never explained, the shopping center allowed a competing franchise, the Burger Doodle, to move in a few doors down. The new franchise began taking sales and my client was not happy. They asked me to bring suit.

Liability was not difficult to establish, but damages were. The Burger Doodle moved in just after my client had added a new children's attraction, which dramatically increased sales. Once the Burger Doodle began operating, sales dropped back almost to the levels experienced before the children's attraction had opened. Our contention was that improper competition from the Burger Doodle had caused lost sales, even though sales were slightly higher than the client's historical average. Their contention was that sales did not decrease from historical averages after the Burger Doodle moved in.

Suddenly, I was immersed in numbers. We had historical sales figures, regional averages, figures for stores with children's attractions, figures for stores without attractions—all kinds of figures. Not surprisingly, my client started sending me spreadsheets. This time, the spreadsheets were in Microsoft's spreadsheet program called Excel, which most of the business world uses.

Fortunately, Excel worked a lot like Quattro Pro, which works a lot like Lotus 1-2-3 for that matter, so it did not take long to get up and running with Excel. I spent a Sunday afternoon watching the Broncos play and brushing up on the few differences between the programs.

Once I was up to speed on Excel, I applied my charting skills to the statistics. The client had provided average sales figures for the Denver regional market along with figures for the store impacted by the new Burger Doodle. The numbers looked promising, but a clear picture emerged when I charted the data.

Figure i: Chart Comparing Monthly Sales

From 2000 to 2005, my client's gross sales had averaged about 15 percent above the Denver market average. When the children's attraction opened, sales shot up dramatically. Then the Burger Doodle opened and sales dropped back to historical averages. Our conclusion was that the Burger Doodle's improper competition took away most or all of the gains resulting from the investment in the children's attraction.

Using the same techniques, I created several other charts: comparing sales by months, comparing sales trends with other stores opening children's attractions, and comparing monthly sales for the store with sales from the previous year. Taken together, they painted a powerful picture of lost sales resulting from improper competition by the Burger Doodle.

While the charting features in spreadsheets first caught my interest, I soon began learning how to use formulas to analyze the numbers in my cases. As you will discover, adding, subtracting, multiplying, and dividing numbers in a spreadsheet is about as simple as working a calculator. To be sure, when you only have two numbers to manipulate, a calculator may be the superior tool. But if you have a series of numbers to analyze, or a series of related calculations to make, the spreadsheet is the better choice. The great strength of a spreadsheet is its ability to manipulate hundreds, even thousands, of numbers with the results of one calculation being used as the basis of another.

I started using spreadsheets to perform basic calculations; for example, adding or multiplying the numbers in two columns and placing the result in a third. From there, it was a small step to learn how to use the SUM formula. This simple device allows you to highlight a series of numbers and display the sum in an adjacent cell on the spreadsheet. It can be extremely handy when you are working on business deals with your client, or when you are trying to work out a settlement.

I soon graduated to using some of Excel's more complex formulas. Excel is a sophisticated financial tool used by accountants, mathematicians, and programmers throughout the world. Not surprisingly, it comes loaded with a host of financial and statistical formulas, more than you or I will ever need to learn. But there are a few that are quite handy for lawyers. I use Excel's prebuilt formulas for calculating averages, the present value of a settlement offer, and, sometimes, the future value of a payment made today. While some of these seem intimidating at first, Excel makes them relatively easy to use, as I will show you in this book.

Later, I learned that Excel could also be used as a database, allowing you to sort and filter your data. In one case, my client was accused of selling buggy software. Exhibit A was a list of more than 140 bugs maintained by the customer during product installation. My task was to try and make sense out of the bug reports, determine which of the bugs were critical, and track any patterns I could find in the data.

Viewing the half-inch thick stack of paper that made up the bug log, the task seemed hopeless. With the help of my expert, I could page through the log, mark bugs as critical or noncritical, and look for obvious patterns. However, I could not do much else with the data, at least in that form.

So I got one of our typists to key the data into a spreadsheet (I did not have access to an electronic copy of the log). From there, I could start classifying the bugs as critical, noncritical, or other. I could also perform date calculations, taking the difference between the date a problem was logged and the date it was resolved. I soon added a column titled Days to Resolve. Excel did the math for me through a simple formula subtracting the Date Resolved from the Date Opened.

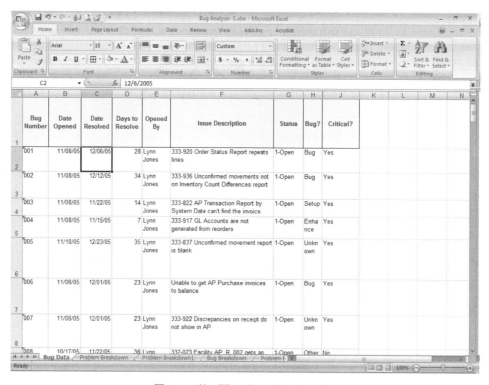

Figure ii: The Bug Analysis

With the data in a spreadsheet, it was a simple matter to sort the bugs according to various criteria—Days to Resolve, Date Opened, Date Closed, Type of Bug, etc. Excel also allowed me to filter the data. This means that Excel hid from view all information that did not meet the criteria I was using. Thus, by using a filter to show critical bugs only, I quickly determined that there were only about 25 critical bugs of the original 140 claimed bugs.

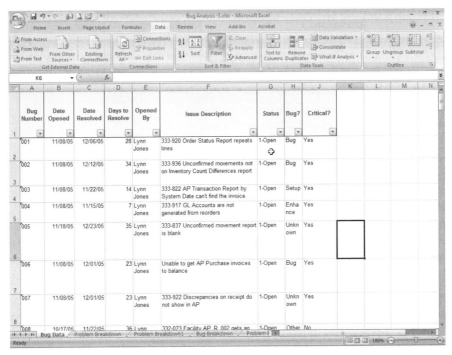

Figure iii: Filtering the Bug Log

Ultimately, I charted the results of my analysis, in this case, demonstrating that of the 140 problems logged, only a small portion consisted of critical bugs. In deposition, their expert had agreed that noncritical bugs did not provide a basis for terminating the software contract.

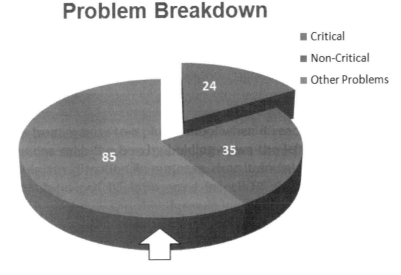

Figure iv: A Beginning Pie Chart

So, why bother with spreadsheets? Because they can be a powerful ally in the practice of law. Whether you are a business lawyer or a trial lawyer like me, you will find spreadsheets to be incredibly handy tools for calculating, sorting, filtering, and charting data. So handy, that every lawyer, in my opinion at least, should know how to use them. Once you do, you will find lots of reasons to put them into action.

I am not suggesting that you will always be the one creating the spreadsheet in the first instance. More often than not, your client or an accountant has created the initial spreadsheet. What you can do is work with the spreadsheet, performing "what if" calculations, modifying formulas, and charting the results. In other cases, you may create the spreadsheet from scratch. Either way, you come out ahead, both in terms of your work product and a suitably impressed client.

This book is designed to teach lawyers how to create and work with spreadsheets. We start from the very beginning. In Lesson 1, I will introduce you to the concept of spreadsheets; explain how rows, columns, and cells work; and teach you how to move around a spreadsheet. You do not need any special knowledge to begin other than a basic facility with Microsoft Windows.

In Lesson 2, we will start working through a simple spreadsheet problem. We will begin to create a Post-Judgment Interest calculator and use it as a vehicle to teach you how to add words and numbers to a spreadsheet and format your data.

In Lesson 3, we begin using simple formulas to calculate data for our spreadsheet. We start with the four types of mathematical calculations: addition, subtraction, multiplication, and division. We will then learn about using references to different cells in our formula (as a better alternative to typing in the numbers themselves). By the end of this lesson, we will have completed our Post-Judgment Interest calculator. This is a handy tool in itself but, more importantly, it provides a springboard for other custom applications you may want to create.

Lesson 4 covers advanced formulas. I will show you how to use the SUM function and, generally, how to execute Excel's built-in formulas. To get you started, I will show you how to calculate averages using Excel's AVERAGE function and how to do present and future value calculations. We will also create a summary spreadsheet using data from other spreadsheets.

The examples in the first four lessons come from my litigation practice. If you are a business lawyer, fear not. The techniques I will cover are equally valuable to your business practice. Whether we are talking about formatting, simple math, or complex formulas, the techniques are the same. It is just a matter of solving a different type of problem.

To prove the point, I will focus on business spreadsheets in Lesson 5. My purpose is twofold: to cap off the first four lessons with some additional examples and to show how useful spreadsheets can be in a business practice.

In Lesson 6, we will discover how Excel can function as a database. Drawing from the case of the "Not-so Buggy Software," I will show you how to display, sort, and filter data. You may never need a database program like Microsoft Access again.

We will chart our data from the Not-so Buggy Software case in Lesson 7. I will show you how to create the pie chart we saw in Figure iv, along with line and column charts. At the end of this lesson, you should know all you need to create sophisticated graphs for trial or for a business presentation.

In our last lesson, I will teach you how to print a spreadsheet. To those familiar with word processors, this may seem anticlimactic. However, there are some tricks to be learned about formatting your spreadsheet and Lesson 7 is well worth taking the time to work through it. After all, if you cannot print or display your work in an attractive fashion, your underlying analysis may lose some of its impact.

I think you will enjoy this book. While there are scads of Excel help books on the market, this one was written by a lawyer for lawyers and other legal professionals. After watching many of my partners scratch their heads as they tried to work through a six-inch manual written by a computer geek, I thought it was time for a tech-savvy trial lawyer to try and simplify things.

I tested this manuscript on many of my colleagues and they have helped me to refine the lessons we will cover. I am hoping that you will be the beneficiary of these efforts. If you work through this book, I promise you will come away the victor. You will be a sophisticated spreadsheet user able to apply this powerful software to all facets of your practice.

As a supplement to the book, we have created a companion CD-Rom attached to the back cover. There you will find copies of the spreadsheets that we work on in this book. You can download them and use them as you work through this book.

I wrote the predecessor to this book in 2000 as *The Lawyer's Guide to Spreadsheets* (Glasser LegalWorks, 2000). This book updates that version for Excel 2007. The examples and the content haven't changed much because the points I was making then apply with equal force now. More to the point, the features and functions that made spreadsheets so powerful then are the same ones that make Excel 2007 so powerful now.

In this book, my goal was to show you how to do many of the same exercises using Excel 2007's new interface. If you are using an earlier version of Excel (2003 for instance) the book will still be useful to you, although you might have to click in different places for some features. But, this isn't a book about the relative features or functionality of different versions of Excel. Rather, it is a book about how useful Excel (or any spreadsheet program for that matter) can be in your practice. So, if you have Excel 2007 so much the better. If you have a different version, I think you will still find the book useful to your practice. At the least, I sure hope you do.

Enjoy the book and let me know what you think.

John Tredennick

The Basics

I assume you have Excel 2007 loaded on your computer or that it is otherwise accessible to you. If so, fire it up. (That is Gen-next speak for start the program.) Then, if it is not open already, open a blank *workbook* as shown in Figure 1-1.[1] In Excel 2007, there are several ways to start a new spreadsheet. The simplest is to click on the round "Office Button" button at the top left-hand corner of your screen and choose New. Or, you can use the standard control keystroke combination Ctrl+N (depress the Ctrl button and the N key simultaneously).

A *workbook* is Excel's term for a file containing one or more *worksheets*, which are more commonly known as *spreadsheets*. The term came from the accounting world and described a large sheet of paper with horizontal and vertical grid lines used to array financial information. Because of its ubiquity and history, I will use the term spreadsheet throughout this book. It is interchangeable with the term worksheet.

In Lesson 1, I will teach you some of the basics about spreadsheets: what they are, how to move around them, and how to move between different spreadsheets. After this brief introduction, we will get down to the business of adding data to spreadsheets.

A spreadsheet can contain various types of information including numbers, text, graphics, and even links to other spread-

---

[1]These screen shots are from my computer and reflect the way I have set up Excel. You may be on a different tab in the "Ribbon" or have Excel set up in a slightly different way so that it looks a bit different than my screen shots. Don't let the differences throw you. The basic functions don't vary much even as the versions change.

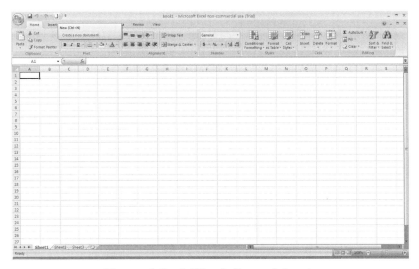

Figure 1-1: A Blank Spreadsheet

sheets, files, or websites. Think of it as a blank sheet of electronic paper, optimized for numeric data rather than words. This is where you will do your work.

Rows, Columns, Cells, and Ranges

Spreadsheets are organized into rows, columns, and cells. Rows are horizontal and each is identified by a number—from row 1 to row 1,048,576. Columns are vertical and each is identified by a letter—beginning with column *A* and continuing to column *XFD* (which is more than 16,000 columns). With Excel 2007, there are far more rows and columns than you will ever need.

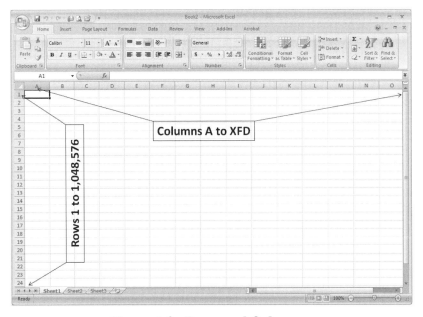

Figure 1-2: Rows and Columns

This business of rows and columns is the genius behind spreadsheets. The box located at the intersection between each row and column is called a *cell*. Thus, a spreadsheet consists of a series of cells, each denominated by its row number and column letter (called a cell address). The first cell in your spreadsheet is called *A1*. Moving to the right, the next is *B1*, then *C1*, and so on, through *XFD*. If you move downward from cell A1, you go to cell A2, and then A3. Eventually, you will reach cell 1,048,576.

A series of cells is called a *range*. Thus, the cells from A2 through A15 comprise a range of cells. In Excel language, you denote the range as *A2:A15*. Or, if the range is horizontal, it would be *A2:D2*. Either way, the term range is a handy way to describe a series of cells.

Moving Around Your Spreadsheet

There are many ways to move around your spreadsheet. Start by clicking on different cells with your mouse. (For example, click on cell D3, which is at the intersection of column D and row 3.) The name of the cell you have chosen appears in the *Name box*, which is at the top left of your screen, just below the menu and toolbars. The Name box is part of the "formula bar," which we will discuss in a later lesson.

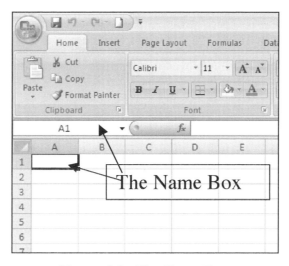

Figure 1-3: The Name Box

A second way to move around is to use the arrow keys on your keyboard. (Make sure the Scroll Lock key is turned off.) Press the appropriate arrow key to move to the right, left, down, or up.

You can move to different portions of your spreadsheet by using the scroll bars located at the right and at the bottom of your screen. Click the triangle arrow above or below the vertical scroll bar to move one row at a time.

Click the space between the triangle and the scroll box, which moves up and down the scroll bar, to move up or down a screen of data. Or, you can drag the scroll box itself. The same process works for the horizontal scroll bar. Use it to move between columns.

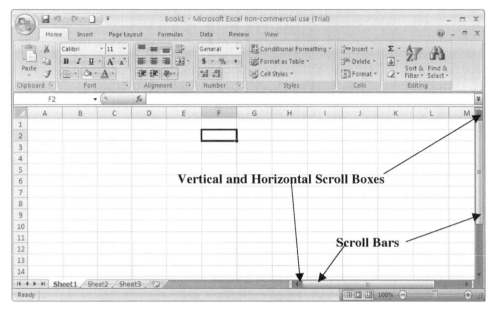

Figure 1-4: Scroll Bars and Scroll Boxes

You can use the Page Up or Page Down keys to move up or down a screen of data. Pressing Ctrl+Home takes you to the top of the spreadsheet. Ctrl+End takes you to the end of your workspace (rather than the end of your spreadsheet).

If you want to move to a specific cell, you can also execute the shortcut key combination Ctrl+G (Go to) and specify the cell address.

Practice moving around your spreadsheet until you are comfortable using the various options.

Moving Between Spreadsheets

One of the great breakthroughs in spreadsheet development was the ability to have more than one spreadsheet in a single file. With Excel, you can have an almost unlimited number of spreadsheets. A formula in one sheet can be linked to data in another, which allows for almost unlimited analytical and presentation possibilities.

This cross-linking capability is central to Excel's utility. I was in charge of a division at my law firm called Trial Partners. It consisted of three groups: Graphics, Litigation Consulting, and Litigation Support. To keep track of the division's financial performance, I used an Excel workbook with each group's financial information kept on a separate spreadsheet. The first spreadsheet provides a summary page with group totals taken from (linked to) other spreadsheets in the workbook. The summary figures update automatically when data in the other sheets change.

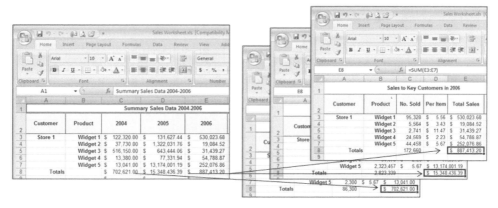

Figure 1-5: Summary Spreadsheet Linked to Detail Sheets

You can move between the different spreadsheets in your workbook by clicking on the tabs located at the bottom of the screen. By default, the tabs on all Excel workbooks are labeled: Sheet1, Sheet2, Sheet3, and so on. Click on different ones to move to different spreadsheets.

If the mouse is not handy, or you prefer using keystrokes, you can move to different spreadsheets in your workbook by pressing Ctrl+PgUp or Ctrl+PgDn. (I can never remember all these shortcut key combinations, so I just use my mouse.)

You can easily rename a spreadsheet to something more descriptive. Right click on any spreadsheet tab and choose Rename from the menu that appears. Other options on this menu can also be handy. The Move or Copy option allows you to reorder the sheets in your workbook. Or, you can move the spreadsheet to a new location by dragging the tab to another location.

Now that we have covered these basic elements of a spreadsheet, it is time to start entering data. That will be the focus of Lesson 2.

Sidebar: Many Ways to Skin a . . .

Like all Windows programs, Excel offers several ways to issue a program command. The menu bar in Excel 2007 is now located within the Office logo at the top left-hand corner of the screen. It can be accessed via the mouse or by pressing the Alt key in conjunction with the underlined letter of the desired menu command. Pressing Alt+F, for example, opens the File menu.

Figure 1-6: The Menu Bar

Excel 2007 has changed the way tool bars work by adding the "Ribbon." Click on the Home menu option to see most of your standard formatting options.

Figure 1-7: The Home Menu with Standard Formatting Options

The menu options you find on the "Ribbon" provide quick access to program commands. If you are not familiar with a particular button, hold the mouse over it briefly and a descriptive message appears.

The third way to access program commands is through a shortcut key combination. Several are prebuilt and are standard throughout Windows. Ctrl+P (pressing the Ctrl button and the P keys simultaneously) is the standard shortcut key command for printing. Ctrl+S is the standard Save command.

By the way, many of these commands whether menu, toolbar, or shortcut keys, can be customized, changed, or even removed. In this book, I will work with Excel commands using standard configurations. If your setup is different, you can make the appropriate adjustments.

Entering Data

The Problem

Memo: To Partners

From: Joe Litigator

Re: Post-Judgment Interest Issue

Our client recently won a $16.1 million judgment for breach of fiduciary duty. The defendant has threatened to appeal if the client does not accept a sharp discount on the judgment. We have advised our client that the judgment will draw 8 percent interest compounded annually throughout the course of the appeal. She has asked me:

(1) What will the judgment be worth in three years after the court of appeals has likely ruled?
(2) What will it be worth in four years, assuming the defendant petitions the Supreme Court and drags things out?; and
(3) What will it be worth in six years, assuming *certiorari* is granted?

We are confident that most of the judgment will be affirmed, but see a possibility that the court will cut out $2 million based on a theory of double recovery. It is also likely that the court will toss out the $2.1 million prejudgment interest award.

I promised the client I would get back to her with interest amounts for each of the periods based on different final judgment amounts. I do not want to hire an accountant to do the math and, besides, I have to call her after lunch. Can anyone help me?

This type of problem is not unusual in a law practice, and it is one I faced several years ago. To solve it, most of us would pull out a calculator or a pencil and paper and start working out the math. In these next two lessons, I want to show you how we can use a spreadsheet to do the job. While the problem is simple enough to do by hand, it provides an ideal training exercise to show you how spreadsheets work. And, once you have learned how to create and manipulate a spreadsheet, you will find it easier and more accurate than your hand calculations. Let's get to it.

Adding Words and Numbers

The first step in creating a spreadsheet is to input the basic data—the words and numbers with which you will be working. Start by clicking on a cell and entering an item of information such as a word or a number. Once you are finished, press Enter. The entry is stored in the cell and your cursor moves down a cell. To move to the right, rather than down, press the Tab or the Right arrow key instead. Try each and see what happens.

To start working on our problem, type the words "Post-Judgment Interest Calculator" in cell A1. Next, type the years "2007" in cell A4, "2008" in cell A5, "2009" in cell A6, and so forth through the year "2013."

In cell B3, type the word "Judgment." In cell C3, the words "Interest Rate." In cell D3, the words "Accrued Interest." In cell E3, the words "Revised Judgment." And in cell F3, the words "Per Diem." Do not worry about formatting yet.

Your spreadsheet should look like this:

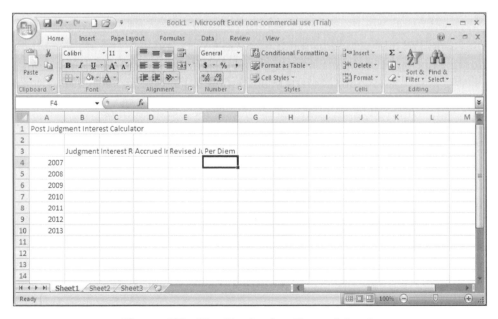

Figure 2-1: The Beginning Spreadsheet

Now is a good time to save your spreadsheet. Choose an appropriate location (directory) on your hard drive, a CD-ROM, USB flashdrive, or a network drive, and save the file. You might name it "Postjudgment Interest Calculator."

Sidebar: Automatic Entry of Numbers and Lists

In this example, we manually typed in the years from 2007 to 2013. With Excel, there is an easier way—Automatic Entry of Numbers and Lists. Here is how it works.

Excel recognizes and can automatically fill in many commonly-used series of numbers or words. In our example, all you need to type in is the first two numbers of the series: 2007 and 2008. After you enter them manually, highlight both by holding down the Shift key as you click on them. It should look like this:

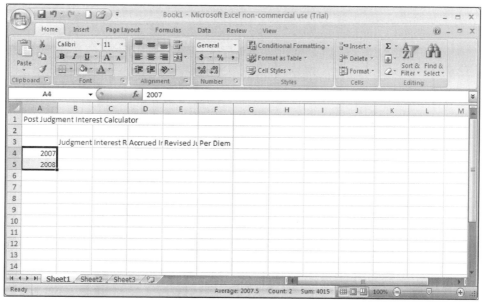

Figure 2-2: Highlighting the Cells

Notice that there is a small box in the bottom right-hand corner of the highlighted cells next to 2008 (cell A5). Excel calls this a *grab handle*. Move your mouse over the grab handle and notice that your cursor has changed from the wide white plus marker to a thin black cross. At this point, you can grab the corner (hold down the left mouse button) and move it downward as far as you need to go. Excel lets you know how far along you are with a helpful tip box to the right of the cursor. It looks like this:

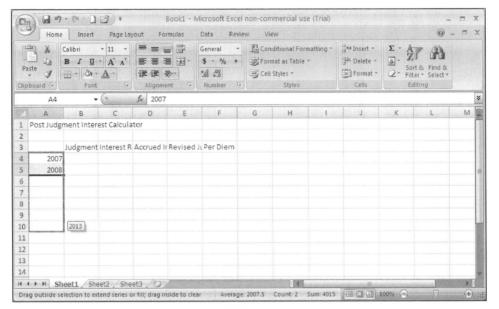

Figure 2-3: Filling In the Series

When you let go of the mouse button, Excel fills in the series. This may not seem like a big deal for the six numbers in our series. But, when you are making a larger spreadsheet, this tool can be very handy.

This AutoFill feature works with almost any combination of numbers, dates, time, and lists that you can imagine. Experiment with it until you are comfortable using it. It is too much of a time-saver for you to ignore.

Formatting Your Data

Our spreadsheet does not look very good at the moment, but at least the basic words and numbers are there. The next step is to format this data.

Excel provides three types of formatting options:

◆ Character formatting;
◆ Number formatting; and
◆ Cell formatting

We will use all three types with our post-judgment interest spreadsheet.

Character Formatting

Character formatting is about making your spreadsheet attractive and more easily understood. You learned character formatting when you learned to use your word processor. As with your word processor, any text or number in your spreadsheet can be boldfaced, italicized, enlarged, etc. If you wanted, each cell in your spreadsheet could have a different font, style, and type size.

Boldfacing, Italicizing, and Font Size

Working on our example, let's start by boldfacing the years in the range 2007 through 2013 (cells A4 through A10). There are a number of ways to accomplish this. You can click on each cell and boldface it individually (by choosing the B button for Bold in the Font section under the Home menu, or by pressing Ctrl+B). A better way to accomplish this task is to select all the cells containing the years first (cells A4 through A10). You can do this by holding down the Shift key as you click the starting and ending cells in the column (or by holding down the left mouse button and dragging over the selected cells). The Bold command would then apply to all of the selected cells.

Here is an even better approach. Click on the column heading for column A. Notice that the entire column is highlighted. Now choose Bold. Your command is applied to every cell in the column. All of the years are boldfaced including the title "Postjudgment Interest Calculator" in cell A1.

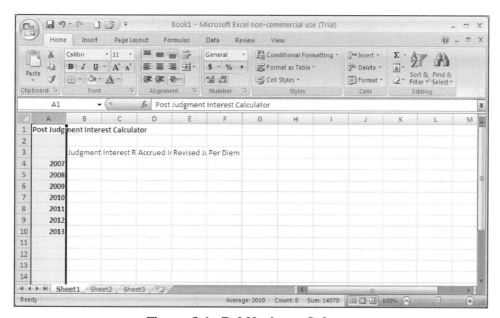

Figure 2-4: Boldfacing a Column

You can do the same with rows. Click on the row heading for row 3. Then choose Bold. All of the entries in row 3 are boldfaced with one keystroke.

In our case, you might have to execute the Bold command twice to get the correct result. If you followed my example, row 3 already had one boldfaced cell—cell A3, which was changed to bold when we boldfaced column A. The rest were not boldfaced. When you click on the Bold command the first time, Excel may actually unboldface cell A3, leaving the other cells alone. Click it a second time, and it boldfaces the row.

Let's work on our spreadsheet heading: "Post-Judgment Interest Calculator." If the heading is not already boldfaced, click on cell A1 and boldface it. Since this is a heading, increase the font size to 14 points and italicize it. As usual, there are lots of ways to do this.

The easiest way is to enter a new font size in the Font section. Click on the Font size box and type a new number, or click on the triangle to the right of the box and select a new font size from the drop-down box. You can italicize the text as well by clicking on the slanted "*I*" button on the toolbar.

As an alternative, select Format from the Cells section (under the Home menu) and choose Format Cells. The Format Cells dialog box appears. To change the font, choose the Font tab at the top of the box. You can change the font style to italics here as well.

As a third alternative, rightclick on the cell and choose the Format Cells option from the menu that appears. The Format Cells dialog box appears.

Sidebar: The Format Cells Dialog Box

The Format Cells dialog box acts as command central for cell formatting. Notice the tabs along the top of the box. By clicking on them, you can choose different kinds of formatting options. Play with the various number options and see what happens to your number.

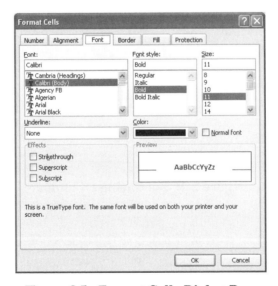

Figure 2-5: Format Cells Dialog Box

The Alignment tab allows you to choose how the number appears in the cell. You can center the number, right or left justify it, or specify that it align with the top, bottom, or middle of the cell. You can also specify Font, Font style, and Size, Borders, and other options, many of which we will cover later.

Merging Cells

While we are at it, let's adjust our spreadsheet title: "Post-Judgment Interest Calculator." Since we want the title to frame the top of our spreadsheet, let's center it between cells A1 and F1. We do this through the Merge cells command. Here is how this useful feature works.

Highlight the applicable cells. Then choose the Merge and Center button on the Alignment section. Or, choose the Alignment tab from the Format Cells dialog box and select the Merge cells checkbox. Now, your text is centered across the merged cells.

The end result of our work so far should look like this:

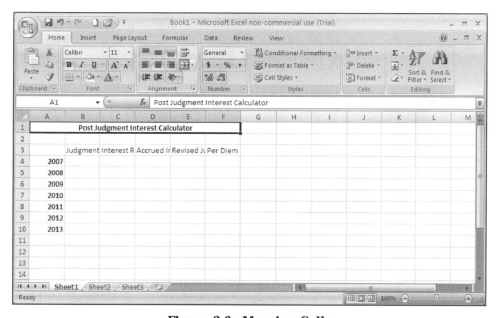

Figure 2-6: Merging Cells

Adjusting Column Width

We have one last character-formatting task. You probably noticed that our headings—Judgment, Interest Rate, Revised Judgment, etc.—are too long for the cells they occupy. Either they run into the next cell or are truncated. There are a couple of ways to fix this problem.

A simple solution is to widen the columns to fit the headers. As usual, there are several ways to do this. One option is to right-click on the column heading and choose the Column Width menu option. To widen the column, use a larger number for its width.

A better option is to use your mouse to widen the column. Move your mouse to the intersection between column headings B and C. Notice that your mouse pointer turns into a double arrow when you reach the column intersection. Hold down the left mouse button and drag the arrow to the right. Notice that column B widens. You can size it to fit the entire word "Judgment."

If you double-click on the intersection between the columns, rather than drag them, the column to the left of the intersection resizes itself to fit the widest entry in the column. This is the easiest way to widen the column to the exact size you need for this problem.

Widen columns C, D, E, and F using whichever technique you prefer. Your spreadsheet should now look like this:

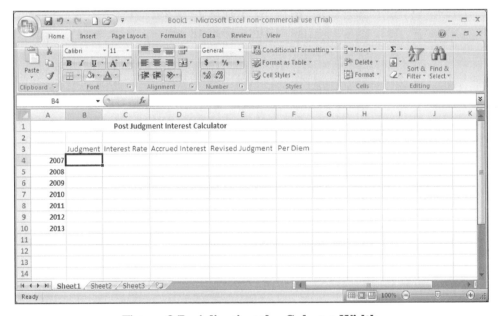

Figure 2-7: Adjusting the Column Width

Sooner or later in the course of entering or calculating numbers, you will run across a cell result that looks like this: "##########." This is Excel's way of telling you that your column is too narrow to display the number in that cell. Make the column wider and the number will display properly.

Text Alignment

There is another option available to you. Instead of widening columns C through F, you can wrap the text in the columns so the headings appear as a stacked entry.

After highlighting cells C3 and D3, open the Format Cells dialog box. Choose the Alignment tab and click on the box next to the *Wrap text* option. If your text is wider than the current column width, Excel displays a multi-line heading. If the text is not wider, as in the case where you have already widened the column to the full width of the text, there is no change. In that case, narrow the column and the text wraps.

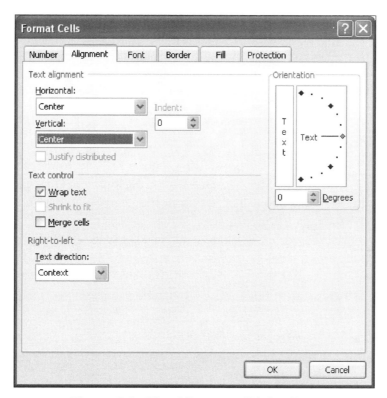

Figure 2-8: The Alignment Dialog Box

There are a number of other handy alignment features. You can center your headings horizontally or vertically, shrink the text size to fit the space allowed, and indent the text. Experiment with these features so that you know what you can do when you need it.

Here is how the wrapped and centered text looks:

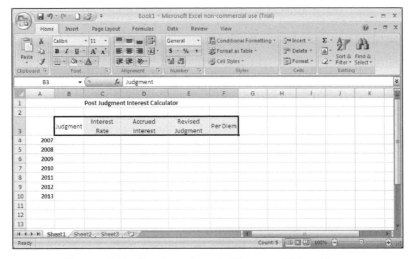

Figure 2-9: Centered and Wrapped Headings

You now know most of what you need to understand about character formatting.

Number Formatting

Excel offers a second kind of formatting, called *number formatting*. Number formatting relates to the type of number we are using: currency, percentages, fractions, etc. Knowing about number formatting can be both a time-saver and an aid when you start using formulas.

Let's start by entering the judgment amount, $16.1 million, into cell B4. Type 16100000 into the cell and press Enter. Do not add commas or the $ sign.

We can now format this number and, in the process, tell Excel what kind of number we are using. Click on the $ button on the toolbar. Excel reformats the number as $16,100,000.00.

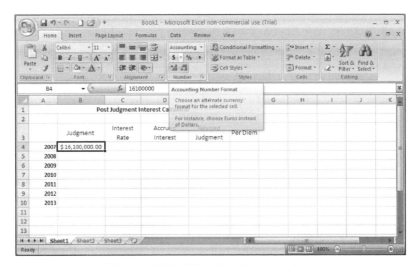

Figure 2-10: Number Formatting

You could also choose to add the $ sign yourself. If you type $16,100,000.00, Excel would treat the number as currency.

You can eliminate the cents display (the two digits to the right of the decimal point) and just show whole dollar amounts. You can do this by either clicking on the Decrease Decimal button on the Number section of the Home toolbar or by selecting no decimals on the Format/Number menu option.

Our next step is to add our post-judgment interest rate of 8 percent. Enter the number *8%* in cell C4. By adding the % sign, you are telling Excel that your number is a percentage. Alternatively, you could have entered the amount .08 and then clicked on the % button on the number section of the Home menu (or chosen Format/Format Cells/Number from the Home menu). It does not matter how you do it as long as Excel knows it is a percentage. Otherwise, your formulas would produce incorrect results.

You can change and control your number formatting through the Format Cells dialog box. Click on the Number tab and you will see all of your options.

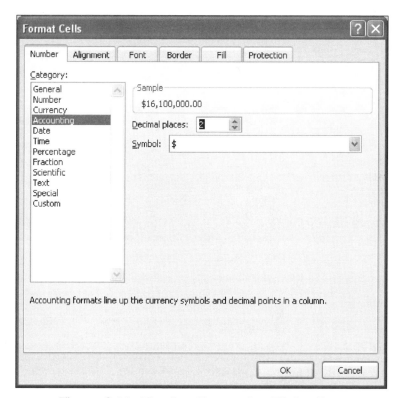

Figure 2-11: Number Formatting Dialog Box

For the most part, all of your options are self-explanatory. Try different ones and see what happens.

Cell Formatting

The last bit of formatting we will learn is *cell formatting*. We use cell formatting to place borders around a cell or group of cells, or to change the color or texture. As with display formatting, we are mostly talking about looks here, but looks can be important.

A few simple examples give you an idea of what can be done. To start, highlight cells B3 through F3. Then click the Down arrow on the Borders button in the Font section of the Home menu, or select the Borders tab in the Cell Format dialog box. Notice the choices for cell borders. Let's choose a simple line around the cells. Like this:

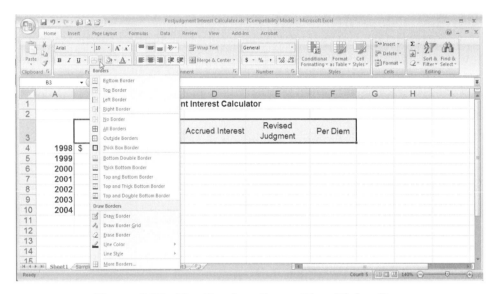

Figure 2-12: The Borders Formatting Dialog Box

To finish our formatting, add a line to the right of cells A4 through A10. Use the same commands to reach this result.

We could also set off the headings with color. Highlight cells B3 through F3 and click on the Fill Color drop-down box, which is also located on the Formatting toolbar. Make the boxes yellow.

There are endless formatting options you can use, but this is enough for our purposes. You now have the beginnings of a working spreadsheet to help us work through our post-judgment interest problem. Our next step is to add the formulas that will help us calculate post-judgment interest. We will do that in Lesson 3.

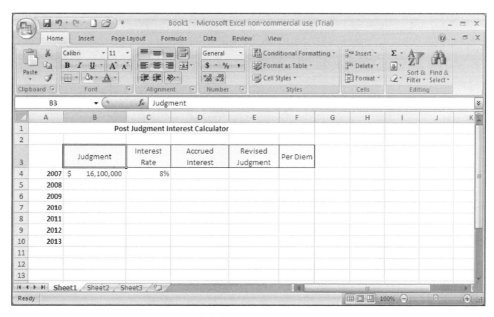

Figure 2-13: Final Formatting

Adding Simple Formulas

Thus far, we have discussed what a spreadsheet is, how to enter basic data, and how to format that data to make it more presentable. Now we get to the heart of what spreadsheets are all about. Here is where we learn about formulas.

The Basics: Addition, Subtraction, Multiplication, and Division

Let's get back to work on our problem. Our client has asked us to determine how much post-judgment interest she would be entitled to on her $16.1 million judgment. In Lesson 2, we set up a basic format for our analysis. Our spreadsheet ended up looking like this:

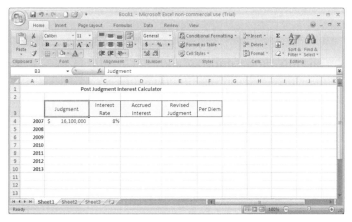

Figure 3-1: The Formatted Spreadsheet

The next step is to determine how much interest will be accrued at the end of the first year of the judgment. Now we get to our first formula.

In our jurisdiction, post-judgment interest is compounded annually. As a result, the interest calculation for the first year is relatively simple: judgment amount times the interest rate. Using our assumed numbers, post-judgment interest for the first year equals $16.1 million times 8%. Total interest for the first year is $1,288,000.00.

Using Excel as a Simple Calculator

We can do the calculation in Excel just as easily as we can with a calculator. Here is how.

Click on cell D4 and press the = (equal) key (or click the = button on the Formula bar). The = key tells Excel you are going to insert a formula into a cell. Your formula follows the = key.

From there, you could treat Excel just like a calculator. Type the following formula in the cell: =16100000*8%, and press the Enter key.[1] Excel multiplies the two numbers together and gives you the result: 1288000.00. Do not worry about formatting the result as currency. We can do that later when we are finished setting up the rest of our spreadsheet.

Using Relative Cell References

Because Excel is more than a fancy calculator, there is a better way to accomplish the same result. Rather than manually entering the numbers in your formula, tell Excel to use the results stored in other cells as the basic building blocks for your formula. In our case, the formula would work like this: =B4*C4. What you are telling Excel to do is multiply the amount in cell B4 ($16,100,000.00) times the amount in cell C4 (8%).

Here is the result:

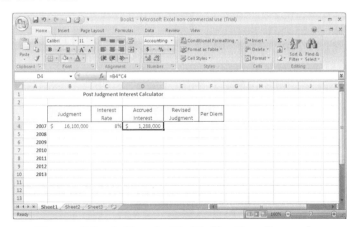

Figure 3-2: A Simple Multiplication Formula

---

[1] Excel does not allow you to use a $ sign or a comma in your formula. If you use these symbols, Excel gives you an error message and offers to reformat your formula. Excel does, however, allow you to use a % sign.

There is a reason why this approach is so important. By using cell references, rather than the numbers themselves, we make it easier to run "what if" scenarios or react to changed data. The power of a spreadsheet is not so much in its ability to do math, but in its ability to link multiple calculations together so it can be automatically updated when any one cell changes its value.

You will quickly see the advantages of this approach even in our simple interest calculator. Our first formula was designed to tell us how much interest would accrue in the first year at an annual rate of 8 percent. What if we wanted to change the rate to 10 percent?

If we use cell references in our formula, we only need to change the value in one cell—cell C4. Because the formula in cell C5 (=B4*C4) is based on cell references rather than specific numbers, the results of our formula are updated automatically. Try it for yourself.

If you use specific numbers for the formula in C5 (=16100000*8%), rather than cell references, you have to change the interest rate information in cell C4 *and* the formula in cell C5 before you can present the results of the changed interest rate. And, if you want to change it back to 8 percent, or try another interest rate, you have to make these changes again.

This may not seem like a big issue with a simple formula like this. But wait until you create a large spreadsheet with formulas spread over many pages. Then the difference becomes all-important. Trust me on this one.

An Easier Way to Enter Cell References

Now that you have mastered the concept of using a cell reference rather than specific numbers, let me show you an easier way to input your formula. Rather than typing the formula =B4*C4, use your mouse to accomplish the same result. Click on cell C5 and press the = key (or click on the = button). Then, using your mouse, select cell B4. Once you have selected it, press the * (star/asterisk) key, and then select cell C4. From there, press the Enter key. Notice that the result of your formula appears, which is the same as if you typed it yourself: =B4*C4.

What is the difference? None, technically. Both accomplish the same result. But typing cell references is tedious and provides an opportunity for errors. I find it much easier to click on the cells I am using in my formula. This is particularly true for more complex formulas or formulas that refer to cells on different pages in your workbook. Once you have mastered both approaches, make your own choice.

Sidebar: More About the Formula Bar

The Formula bar provides you with a handy way to see both your formula and its results. In Figure 3-2, you can see the formula =B4*C4 in the Formula bar. You can see the result $1,288,000.00 in cell D5.

The Formula bar is a legacy of the first DOS-based spreadsheets such as Lotus 1-2-3 and VisiCalc. In those days, all of your input and editing had to be done in the Formula bar, and you could not make entries directly in a cell. Today, Windows-based spreadsheets offer the option of "in-cell" editing. You can input information directly in the cell itself, or you can input it in the Formula bar window after you select the cell.

If you want to edit a formula, you still have both options. Click anywhere within the formula displayed in the Formula bar window and make your change. Or, double click the cell itself and the formula appears. From there, you can make the necessary change. Either way, the result is the same.

More Simple Formulas

Let's continue adding the formulas for columns E and F. By the time we are through with this spreadsheet, you will understand most of what you need to know about formulas.

The column "Revised Judgment" is meant to reflect the new amount of the judgment, which includes accrued interest, at the end of the year. Its formula is simple. Add the amount of the judgment at the beginning of the year to the amount of post-judgment interest accrued in that year. In numerical terms, it is the sum of $16,100,000.00 + $1,288,000.00.

Here is the same formula using cell references: =B4+D4. In English, we are adding the sum of cell B4 ($16,100,000.00) plus the sum of cell D4 ($1,288,000.00). Using the alternative point and click method I showed you, click on cell E4, then press the = key to tell Excel that you are going to use a formula. From there, click on cell B4, press the + (plus) key, click on cell C4 and press Enter. With either approach—typing the formula manually or using the point and click method—the revised judgment amount is $17,388,000.00. (Remember: if you get ##### in cell E4, double click on the line between column heading E and F to widen your column.)

In the hope this is making sense to you, let's tackle our last column: "Per Diem Interest." The purpose of this column is to give you a daily post-judgment interest amount. It will be useful if you ever need to determine how much interest is owed at the end of a partial-year period.

Our formula for per diem interest is: Accrued Interest (the amount of post-judgment interest earned over the year) divided by 365 days.[2] In Excel terms, our formula is simply: =D4/365, which comes to about $3,500.00.

Here are the results of our two additional calculations:

---

[2] I do not want to get sidetracked over whether to use a 360 or a 365-day year. This is a book about spreadsheets, not financial calculations. I will show you how to set up and calculate formulas. You will have to determine the correct formula for your particular purpose.

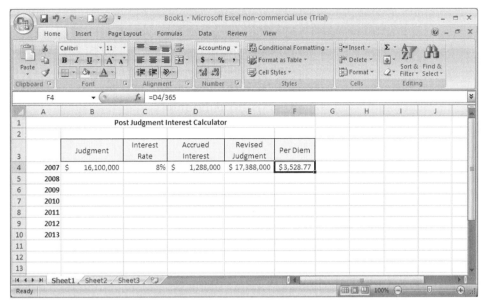

Figure 3-3: Two Additional Formulas

Let's review our progress. We have now worked through many of the basic formulas you will need for your practice. Adding, subtracting, multiplying, and dividing are simple processes with Excel. Your formula begins with an = sign, and then consists of cell designations (or numbers), and the appropriate mathematical command.

Here are the four basic mathematical formulas. They should make sense to you now.

=B1+C1: Add the amounts in cells B1 and C1.

=B1-C1: Subtract the amount of cell C1 from B1.

=B1*C1: Multiply cell B1 times C1.

=B1/C1: Divide the amount in B1 by the amount in C1.

Grouping and Ordering Formulas

When your formulas get more complicated, you can use parentheses to group or order the calculations. Here is an example. Let's say we want to multiply cell A1 times the sum of cells B1 and C1. Without parenthesis, the formula might look like this:

=A1*B1+C1

Because Excel works from left to right, it provides the wrong result. Excel multiplies cell A1 times cell B1 first and then adds the result to the value of cell C1.

To avoid this problem, use parentheses. Here is how the formula should look:

=A1*(B1+C1)

Excel interprets your formula as a requirement to add the values in cells B1 and C1 and multiply the result by cell A1

Linking and Copying Formulas to Other Cells

Now that we have learned how to use basic formulas to calculate accrued interest, a revised judgment amount, and a per diem rate, let's fill out the rest of the rows of our spreadsheet.

In cell B5, we need to insert the value of the revised judgment because that amount provides the basis for the next year's interest calculation. One way to do it would be to type in the amount $17,388,000.00 manually. A better approach is to tell Excel to use the amount in cell E4 as the value in cell B5. That way, if the amount in cell E4 ever changes (because, for example, we decided to experiment with different interest rates or judgment amounts) the amount in cell B5 would automatically reflect the revised judgment amount as well.

Here is the simple formula to place in cell B5: =E4. This formula tells Excel to place whatever value it finds in cell E4 into cell B5. The result looks like this:

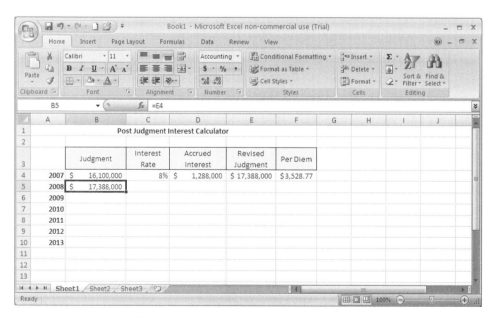

Figure 3-4: Referring to Other Cells

Sidebar: Linking Cells Dynamically

This is the real genius of spreadsheets and the reason why they are so much more useful than calculators. You can build incredibly complex spreadsheets with dynamically-linked cells so the results in one cell provide data for a calculation made in another cell. By changing a key number, such as an interest rate, you can revise other calculations in an electronic ripple effect.

At the ABA TECHSHOW several years ago, Jim Manzi asserted that his spreadsheet, Lotus 1-2-3, made the takeover binge of the 1980s possible. Suddenly, financiers had the power to run complex "what if" financial scenarios in seconds. They could see the impact on a company's financials of different cash payouts, interest rates, etc. It enabled them to fine-tune their deals by the minute without need for a team of accountants to run the numbers.

All of this stems from the ability to link spreadsheet cells together. By changing one value, you can change them all.

Our next step is to insert an interest rate in cell C5. Rather than type in 8 for 8 percent, tell Excel to use the value for cell C4 (=C4). That way, if you decide to try a different interest rate, your calculations in row 5 will be updated as well.

We already know the formula to determine accrued interest for the next year—Revised Judgment times the Interest Rate, or B5 times C5. Rather than retyping the formula, I will show you an easier way to achieve the same result. Click on cell D4 and choose Edit>Copy from the menu bar, or Copy from the toolbar, or use the shortcut key combination Ctrl+C. Then paste the formula in cell D5 using the menu command Edit>Paste, or the Paste icon, or the shortcut key command Ctrl+V.

An interesting thing just happened. The formula in cell D4 was =B4*C4. When you pasted that formula in cell D5, it changed to =B5*C5. How come?

Excel anticipated that you wanted the formula in cell D5 to use data taken from row 5 rather than row 4. So it changed the formula from =B4*C4 to =B5*C5. In our case, that is exactly what we wanted to happen. The formula to determine the accrued interest for 2008 is a function of the amount of the revised judgment at the beginning of 2008 (cell B5) times the interest rate in effect for that year (cell C5).

Let's try that same trick with cell E5, which is the formula for the amount of the revised judgment at the end of 2008. The formula we need to use is Judgment plus Accrued Interest. If we enter the formula manually, we type: =B5+D5. Instead, click on cell E4, copy it, and paste it into cell E5. You get the same result with less typing. Excel automatically transposes the formula in cell E4 (which was B4+D4) into the proper formula for cell E5 (which is B5+C5).

Now try it with the formula for per diem interest. Copy the formula in cell F4 and paste it into cell F5. Your revised formula will be =D5/365, which correctly divides the amount of the revised judgment at the end of 2008 by 365.

Excel calls these *Relative Cell References*. When you copy a formula containing cell references and paste it into another cell, Excel assumes that you intend to refer to other cells holding the same relative position to your target cell (the one in which you are entering a formula) as the original reference cells had to the original target cell containing the formula being copied. In other words, if the formula for C3 is A3*B3—and you copy that formula to cell C4—Excel assumes you meant to change the cell references to A4*B4.

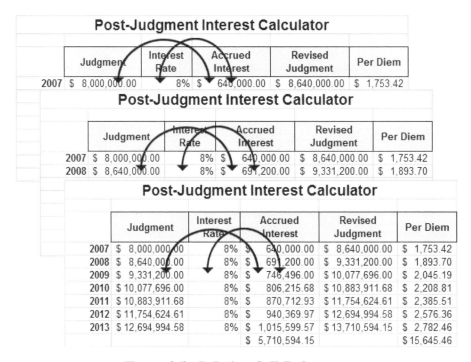

Figure 3-5: Relative Cell References

This is a difficult concept, but an important one for you to master. Let's try a few examples to help you get the hang of it.

Original Formula	New Formula	Comments
E2=D2+A2	E3=D3+A3	The relative references remain in the same column but are dropped down one cell.
F5=G5/C5	F9=G9/C9	You can paste your formula several rows down (or up) and it still maintains the relative references, i.e., the results for cell F9 equal the value in the cell one column to the right divided by the value of the cell three columns to the left.

Original Formula	New Formula	Comments
F5=D4/C4	F8=D7/C7	Notice that the relative reference feature works even if the original references are not on the same row as the results cell. In this case, Excel changes the formula to refer to cells D7 (one column to the right and one row up) and C7 (two columns to the right and one row up).
F5=D4/C4	G5=E4/C4	The relative reference feature works even if you copy your formula to a different column. Excel looks for the proper cells having the same relative position to the new formula cells as the original ones had to the original formula cell.

The bottom line is that Excel is making an assumption—that you intend the cell references to be relative. Most of the time, it is correct. In those few cases where you do not want to use relative references, see the sidebar on using "Absolute Cell References" on page 32.

A Slick Method for Copying the Rest of the Formulas

We now have two rows of the formulas in our post-judgment interest calculator completed. That leaves us with five more rows to complete.

While you could continue cutting and pasting for each of the cells, there is a better way to accomplish the same result. Once you learn it, you will have most of the skills you need to make powerful formula-based spreadsheets.

We are going to drag the formulas into the remaining cells. We do so using the grab handle that is at the bottom, right corner of your highlighted cell or cells.

Click on cell B5. Move your mouse over the box and notice that the cursor changes from a cross to a plus symbol when it reaches that corner. Once it does, you can grab the box by holding down the left mouse key. You can then drag it in any direction. In our case, drag it down one cell. When you let go, the formula in cell B5 is inserted in cell B6 (with the cell references changed appropriately). Thus, the formula in cell B5 =E4 is changed in cell B6 to =E5 to reflect Excel's assumption that you wanted the formula in cell B6 to refer to a cell one row lower than cell E4. That assumption is correct in our case.

Try the same technique for cells C6, D6, E6, and F6. Watch how the formulas from cells C5 through F5 are transposed to refer to the correct cells for the formulas in row 6.

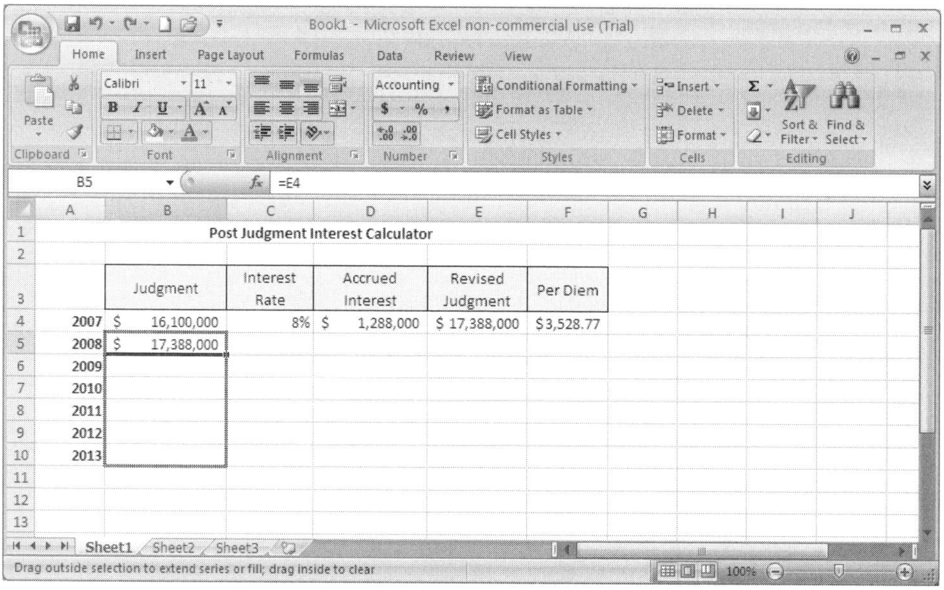

Figure 3-6: Dragging Formulas Using the Grab Handle

Let's move on to row 7, and I will show you a trick to really speed up the process. Start by clicking on cell B6, but do not stop there. Also highlight cells C6 through F6. You can use your mouse to accomplish this (click on cell C6, hold down the left mouse button and drag it to [or click on] cell F6). Or, you can use the keyboard (click on cell C6, hold down the Shift key and use the Right arrow key to move to cell F6).

Once you have the cells highlighted, notice that the grab box appears at the bottom right-hand corner of the highlighted block. Grab it (holding down the left mouse button) and move the mouse down to row 10. Release the left mouse button and voila, all of the proper formulas have been filled in for you. This same technique works with hundreds of rows of formulas. It is a real time-saver.

The Final Step: Formatting Your Results

Now that we have finished our formulas, let's apply some of the formatting tricks we learned in Lesson 2 to finish our chart.

It is pretty easy. Click on the header for column B to select the entire column. Then click on the $ button on the toolbar. The entire column is formatted as currency. If you want to hide the cents and show only whole dollars, click on the Decrease Decimal button, which is just to the right of the $ button. (Recall that you can also execute the Format Cells command from the Menu bar or right click after selecting the column and make the same choice.)

Select column C and choose the % button. The entire column is formatted as a percentage (if it is not so formatted already). For your last step, select columns D, E, and F at the same time by holding down the Ctrl key as you select each column.[3] Then choose the $ formatting button on the toolbar. All of the columns are now formatted as currency.

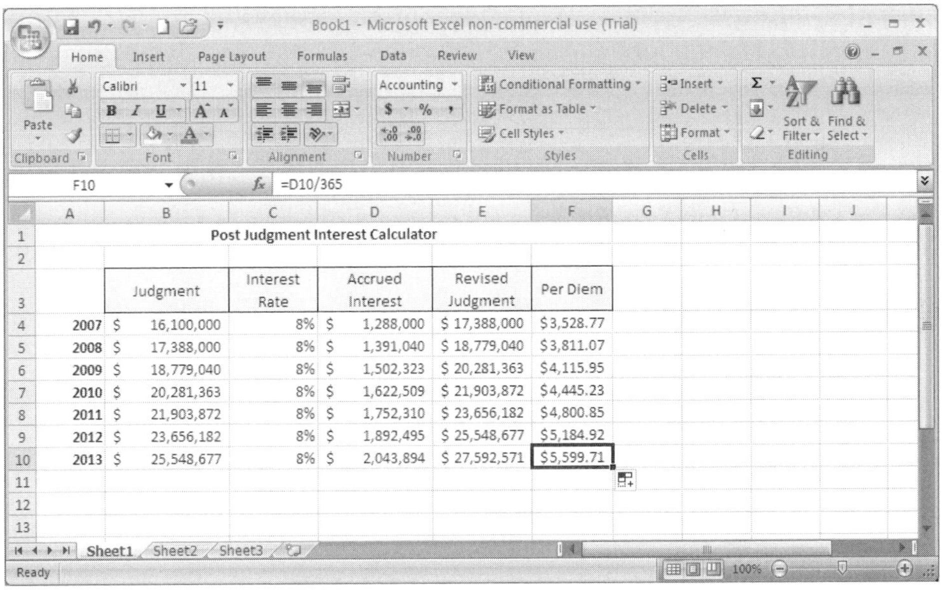

Figure 3-7: The Final Results

Now we have a workable post-judgment interest calculator and we can answer our client's questions. See if you get the same results:

1. What will the judgment be worth in three years, after the court of appeals has ruled?
   Answer: $20,281,363
2. What will the judgment be worth in four years, assuming someone petitions the Supreme Court and that drags things out?
   Answer: $21,903,872
3. What will the judgment be worth in six years, assuming *certiorari* is granted?
   Answer: $25,548,676

---

[3]The Shift key does not work in this instance because we have merged the cells in row 1. If you hold down the Shift key while selecting more than one column, in this instance, Excel highlights the entire merged area.

4. What would the judgment be worth in three years if it is reduced by
   $2 million or $4.1 million?
   Answer: $17,761,939 and $15,242,515, respectively (which we get by
   replacing $16.1 million in cell B4 with $14.1 million or $10 million).

We have now answered our client's question and learned the basics of
spreadsheet formulas in the process. In the next lesson, we will learn about
some more-advanced formulas and make our post-judgment interest calculator a bit more elegant and functional in the process.

Advanced Sidebar: Using Absolute Cell References

In some formulas, you might want Excel to use absolute rather than relative
cell references. That way, when you copy the formula to another cell, the
components of the formula continue to refer to the original cells. Let me explain the concept through an example.

Our post-judgment interest calculator is repetitive in one respect,
namely in the repeat use of 8 percent, the post-judgment interest rate. Since
the interest rate does not change over the course of the calculations, we
could build our spreadsheet without using a separate (repetitive) column
for the 8 percent interest rate. Instead, we could create a separate cell to
hold the interest rate value and let the formulas in each of our rows refer to
that one cell.

Here is how to build our interest calculator using this approach:

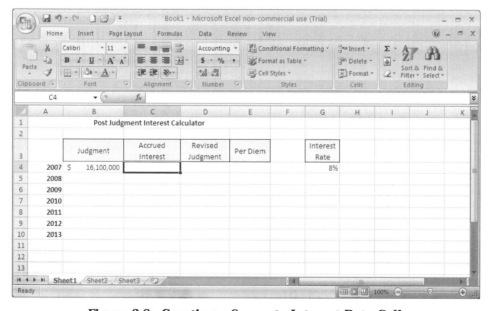

Figure 3-8: Creating a Separate Interest Rate Cell

The formula for cell C4 is still the amount of the judgment times the interest rate. But, in this case, since the interest rate is stored in cell G4, the formula is =B4*G4.

This time, if we use our trick to copy the formula in cell C4 to cell C5—which we need to do in order to calculate the accrued interest for 2008—we have a problem. Excel assumes that you intend to use a relative cell reference in your formula. As a result, the copied formula becomes =B5*G5. Since you have copied your formula to a cell one row down from B4, Excel assumes you intend for that formula to refer to cells one row down from the original cells in the formula. In other words, it assumes you intend to refer to cell B5, which is one row down from cell B4, and to cell G5, which is one row down from cell G4.

Excel has it half right. We want it to use cell B5 in our new formula, but we do not want it to use cell G5. That cell reference should stay the same, pointing to the value in cell G4, no matter how many times we copy the formula.

There is a simple solution to this problem. Use an absolute cell reference in your formula. That tells Excel that your formula must always point to a specific cell, regardless of where it might be copied in your spreadsheet.

Excel uses the $ sign to denote an absolute cell reference. In our example, the formula we need to preserve our absolute reference to the interest rate cell, cell G4 is this: =B4*$G$4. By using $ signs in our formula, we are telling Excel that our formula for accrued interest equals the value in cell B4 (the amount of the judgment) times the value in cell G4 (interest rate). But, by adding the dollar signs to our reference to cell G4, we also tell Excel that if our formula is ever copied, it should always use the value in cell G4 for the interest rate component of the formula.

Thus, when we copy the formula through the remaining rows of our spreadsheet, Excel uses relative references for the portion of the formula that refer to the judgment amount at the beginning of each year, which is correct. But it uses an absolute reference to cell G4 for that portion of each formula, which refers to the interest rate. As a result, you can calculate the interest accruing from different interest rates simply by inserting different values in cell G4. Try it yourself.

You might wonder why we have to insert two $ signs in our cell references. Excel is sufficiently flexible that it can treat either the column or row reference as absolute. Thus, your formula could be =B4*G$4 or =B4*$G4. In the first case, you would be telling Excel to hold the reference to row 4 in the formula as absolute (even though the column reference could vary). In

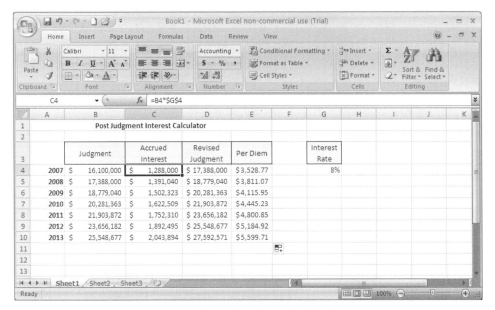

Figure 3-9: Using Absolute Cell References

the second example, you would be telling Excel to hold the column reference G as absolute (although the row reference could vary).

I could probably think of an example where a split reference might be helpful, but I have never needed to use it and you probably will not either. I just wanted you to know why you need to use two $ signs in an absolute cell reference. That is all you need to know for our purposes.

Advanced Formulas and Other Tricks

In Lesson 3, I showed you how to build several basic mathematical formulas. I did that for two reasons. First, you will use these simple formulas over and over as you begin integrating spreadsheets into your practice. Second, it offers a foundation for understanding how to use Excel's more-advanced features.

In this lesson, I will introduce you to some of Excel's built-in formulas, which Excel calls *functions*. We will also cover some more-advanced techniques for setting up your spreadsheets. At the end of this lesson, you will know all you need to set up powerful, highly useful spreadsheets. You will be surprised at how simple they are to create and use in your practice.

The SUM Function

One of Excel's most useful built-in functions is the SUM function. It provides the sum of any series of cells you select. The results are dynamic. If the value of one of the selected cells changes, the calculated sum changes to reflect the new value.

Let's return to our post-judgment interest calculator for one last time to see how the SUM function works. Recall that by the end of Lesson 3, we had created this spreadsheet:

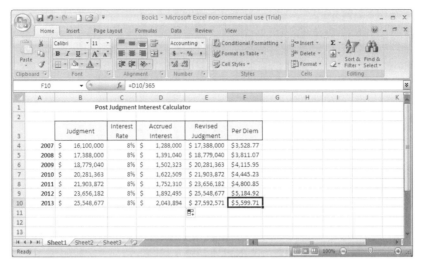

Figure 4-1: The Post-Judgment Interest Calculator

Suppose we wanted to know how much interest had accrued over the entire seven-year period? With Excel, we can easily create a formula to add up the yearly amounts in column D.

Just for practice, try creating this formula yourself. One simple way to do this is to input the formula: =D4+D5+D6+D7+D8+D9+D10. In plain English, I asked Excel to tell me the sum of cells D4 through D10. The result is $8,637,273.65. (Remember, you can accomplish the same result using your mouse. Just click on the cells in your formula using the + key between clicks.)

Excel's SUM function provides a quicker way to reach the same result. Instead of adding each cell in our series, we can tell Excel to sum a range of cells. In this case, we are asking for the sum of the range D4 through D10. In Excel's vocabulary, the formula looks like this:

=SUM(D4:D10)

Excel's way to express a range of cells is through a colon. So, in Excel terms, the phrase D4:D10 means all of the cells from D4 through D10 inclusive.

Most of us do not want to have to remember or even understand formulas like these. The good news is that Excel does not require it. There are two simple ways to execute the SUM function and neither requires you to remember the formula.

The first and best way to sum a series of cells is to highlight all of the cells plus one. By that, I mean highlight all of the cells that contain data to be included in the sum *plus* one additional blank cell. The additional blank cell contains the results of your SUM function.

Once you have highlighted the proper cells, click on the SUM button in the editing section under the Home menu. The SUM button looks like this: Σ.

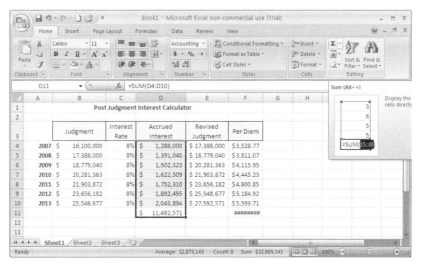

Figure 4-2: The AutoSum Feature

Excel knows that you want the results of the SUM formula to appear in the last blank cell. It will do so with no formula or other typing required.

There is a second way to create a sum. Excel has become so sophisticated that you do not even need to highlight all of the cells being summed. Instead, click on an empty cell at the bottom of a row of numbers, click on the SUM button, and watch what happens. Excel is smart enough to assume that you want to sum the column or row of numbers adjacent to the empty cell. It shows you the cells being summed, then you just press Enter to confirm Excel's choice.

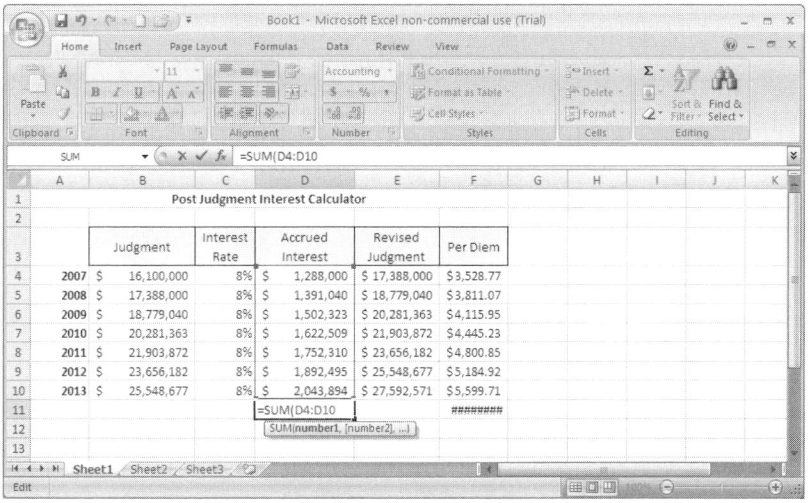

Figure 4-3: Another Way to Create a Sum

As a third approach, you can highlight those cells that contain the numbers you want to sum without adding the blank cell. As long as there is a blank cell next to the series, Excel assumes you want to use it when you execute the SUM function.

You can create sums in any direction—down, up, left, and right. All you need to do is highlight a series of numbers, include a blank cell at the end of the series, and click the SUM button.

Using the Formula Bar

I told you there was a second way to access the SUM function without knowing the formula. This way is through the Formula bar itself. While you will not often use it for simple sums (because the SUM button is so handy), you will need it for other functions you use. So this is a good opportunity to show you how it works.

Click in cell D11 and press the = key. Remember that the = key tells Excel that you are using a formula. Notice that the Formula bar has changed. Instead of seeing the cell name in the left part of the box, now one of Excel's pre-built functions appears, possibly the SUM function. This button is called the Functions button.

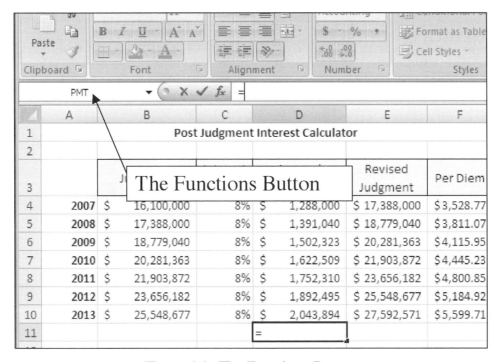

Figure 4-4: The Functions Button

Click on the Down arrow next to the Functions button. A list of commonly used functions along with an option to see More Functions appears. Click this option and explore the many functions available in Excel. Most of them, you will probably never use.

Now let's click on the SUM function button. Excel displays a formula dialog box that looks like this:

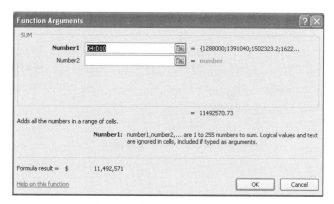

Figure 4-5: The SUM Function Dialog Box

Already, Excel has filled in the proper formula for summing rows D4 through D10, which are the cells we intended to sum. If you are not satisfied with Excel's choice, you have several other options. First, you can type in the formula yourself. Second, you can type each cell's name as a separate number (Excel automatically increases the number boxes as you enter new values.)

Or, best of all, there is a third option. Click on the red arrow button (pointing to miniature cells) to the right of the number box. Immediately, the formula dialog box collapses out of view. Now, click on and highlight the cells you want to use in your formula. When you are finished, press Enter and the Formula dialog box returns. If you are satisfied that you have selected all of the relevant cells, choose OK. Your SUM formula has been entered into the cell.

Using Other Advanced Functions

Excel has lots of other useful functions. While I cannot begin to cover them all (there are big thick books for that), I can point to several and show you how they work. In addition, by showing you how easy these are to use, I hope to also convince you that you can master other functions simply by trying them out, clicking on the Help button, or buying one of the many Excel help books on the market.

Calculating Averages

After calculating sums, one of the most useful functions is the one for calculating averages. Here is how to calculate an average with Excel.

Let's continue with our post-judgment interest calculator. This time, instead of determining the total amount of interest earned over the seven-year period, let's determine the average amount of interest earned each year.

This is a relatively easy calculation, much like calculating sums. The mathematical formula is the sum of cells D4 through D10 divided by seven—the number of cells being considered (in the range).

We can make this calculation a number of ways. Choose a cell to house the results of our formula. Let's try cell D12. We can start with the most basic and later move to more-advanced approaches. Here are several formulas you should now be able to decipher.

The Basic Approach: D12=(D4+D5+D6+D7+D8+D9+D10)/7

Notice the use of parenthesis. In Lesson 3, I showed you how to use parenthesis to group calculations. In this case, Excel adds the values of cells D4 through D10 before dividing the total by 7.

Slightly More Advanced Approach: D12=SUM(D4:D10)/7

This time, we take advantage of Excel's SUM function to add cells D4 through D10 first. Then we tell Excel to divide the result by 7. You can combine functions in formulas almost any way you like.

Excel's Average Function

Rather than figuring out the formula yourself, use Excel's AVERAGE function. It works exactly like the SUM function but performs a different calculation. Here is how it works.

Click on cell D12. Press the = key (or click on the = button) and then click on the Function dialog box. Scroll down to the formula marked AVERAGE. If it is not on the short list presented by Excel, choose the More Functions option. Among other places, it is listed under the Statistical functions.

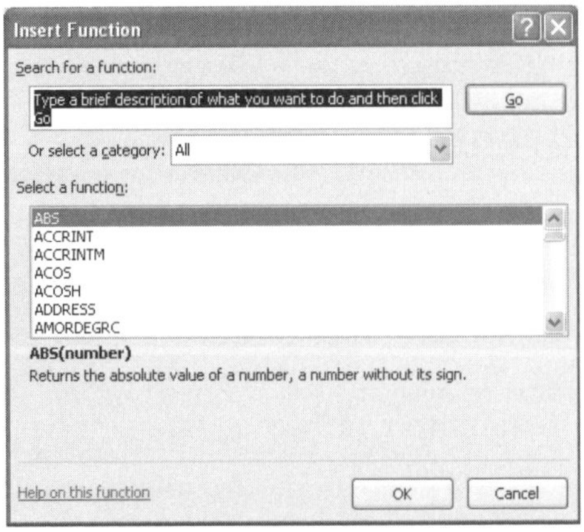

Figure 4-6: The Functions Dialog Box

When you choose the AVERAGE function, a dialog box that looks much like the SUM function dialog box appears.

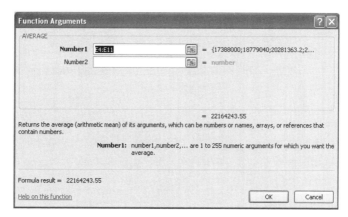

Figure 4-7: The Average Calculator

From here, it should be easy. As with the SUM function, you can type in the numbers manually, indicate a range of numbers to be averaged, or click on the red arrow box and choose the cells to be averaged from your spreadsheet. When you are finished, click OK, and your job is done.

Present Value (PV) Calculations

Most lawyers need to make present value calculations at one time or another. The question comes up for me as a litigator all the time. The defendant is ready to settle but can not pay me now, or needs to pay the settlement over time. How do I evaluate the offer?

You could leave this to your client or call an accountant. But why not use Excel? Now that you are becoming familiar with the program, let's try the present value (PV) function.

Here is the hypothetical. The defendant offers to settle for $100,000.00, payable over 20 months at $5,000 per month. Payments are scheduled for the beginning of the month. What is that worth today, using 8 percent (which is approximately .667 percent on a monthly basis) as my current annual interest rate?[1]

Let me set up the problem in the form of a simple spreadsheet using the simple techniques we learned in Lessons 1, 2, and 3. By now, you should be able to set one up like this with no help from me.

---

[1]Present and future value calculations turn on the interest rate chosen. In this book, I will show you how to use these functions. You (or your client) will have to determine the appropriate discount rates for your situation.

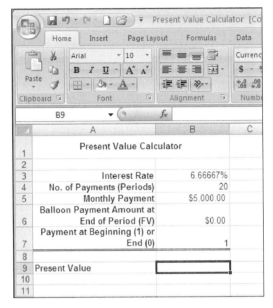

Figure 4-8: Present Value Spreadsheet

Click on cell B9 and then press the = key to start the formula process. Then find the PV function, which may be on the drop-down menu or, if not, it is under the Financial functions category. You should see something like this (you can grab and drag the formula box to another part of your screen):

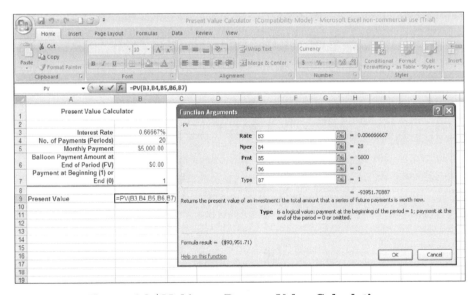

Figure 4-9: Making a Present-Value Calculation

From here, it is just a matter of filling in the boxes (and knowing what information is needed for each box). And, if you don't know, or have forgotten what goes where, click the Help menu. Excel's Help system is, in a word, helpful. Too many people overlook it.

As I have shown you in previous examples, there are several ways to fill out the boxes. The first is the manual approach. Using it, type in the following:

Rate (Interest Rate per Period):	8%/12 (8 percent is the annual rate but we are using monthly periods so we divide by 12)
NPer (Number of periods or payments):	20
Pmt (Payment amount)	$5,000
FV (Amount of a balloon payment at the end)	$0
Type (Payments at the beginning of the month—"1" or the end—"0" or leave blank):	Enter "1"

Let me show you a better way to accomplish the same result. Instead of typing in all the information, click on the appropriate cell references. For the interest rate, click on the red arrow box, collapse the Function dialog box, and choose cell B3. Press Enter to complete your selection. For the number of periods, repeat the same steps but choose cell B5. For the payment amount, repeat the steps and choose cell B4, and for the future value, cell B6.

When you press Enter for the last time, the present value of the payment stream appears, which is $93,329.51. Notice that Excel uses a negative number for the result. This means that you would have to pay someone (like a bank) this amount to purchase the future stream of payments.

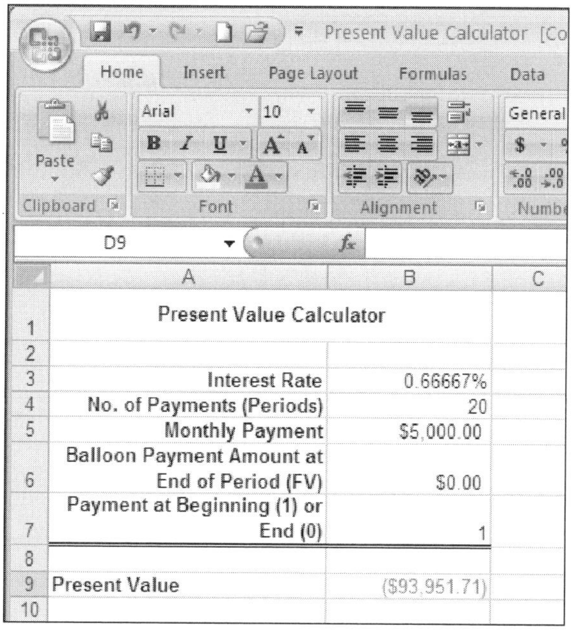

Figure 4-10: The Completed Present-Value Calculation

The benefit of cell references over manually typed values cannot be over-stated. With cell references, we can experiment with different values simply by typing them into the appropriate cell. If we type in the values manually, we have to edit the formula each time.

Try this yourself.

Change the assumed interest rate to 10 percent. The present value is re-duced to $91,000.

Instead, change the payments to $7,000 per month. The present value rises to $130,000.

Change the type of payment from the end of the month to the beginning. Notice the value doesn't change much.

Better than a calculator, we now have a handy tool to analyze different settlement possibilities.

Future Value (FV) Calculator

Future value calculations are not as common as present valuations, but the function is just as simple to use. Let's work through an example.

Rather than future payments, say the defendant owes your client for the future education costs (e.g., college tuition) for a child. The defendant is will-ing to settle now, both to get this dispute over with and also (possibly) to qualify for a tax deduction. What amount must your client receive today to cover $100,000 in college costs ten years from now?

Here is my spreadsheet to answer this question. It is only a slight modi-fication from our present value calculator spreadsheet.

Let me again work through the variables for our calculation. First, select cell E4, press the = key or button, and select Future Value from the Function dialog box (FV in the Financial functions). You can then enter the appropriate information (shown on the following table) or, better yet, select the appropri-ate cells from your spreadsheet.

Rate (Interest Rate per Period):	8 percent (In this case, we are deal-ing with years rather than months.)
NPer (Number of periods or payments):	10
Pmt (Payment amount)	$0 (There are no regular payments in this scenario.)
PV (Amount of the settlement being offered today)	($50,000.00)—the negative number means it is money you are receiving.
Type (Payments at the beginning of the month—"1" or the end—"0" or leave blank):	Because no payments are being received, this is irrelevant to the outcome.

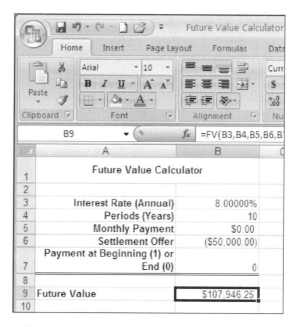

Figure 4-11: A Future Value Calculation

And there you have it. You now know that a settlement payment of $50,000 would be worth about $108,000 in ten years if it is invested at 8 percent.

To check your work, you can run the same scenario as a present value calculation. The question to be answered is: What is the present value of a

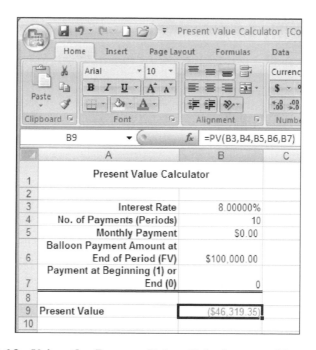

Figure 4-12: Using the Present Value Calculator to Check Results

single payment of $100,000 received ten years in the future with an 8 percent assumed interest rate? My calculation is shown in Figure 4-12, this time using the Present Value Calculator.

Now that you have two useful calculators, you are free to experiment with different interest rates, different settlement amounts, or even a combined payment scheme.

Using Cell References from Different Spreadsheets

The cell references you use in these formulas do not have to be in the same spreadsheet. Excel allows you to refer to cells on different spreadsheets in the same workbook or to spreadsheets in different workbooks. Indeed, Excel lets you refer to data in different types of programs such as databases, but that is beyond the scope of this book.

The option to refer to different worksheets allows you to create summary pages for other spreadsheets. Say, for example, you are tracking sales figures for different customers and different years. Your client has been sued for wrongful sales to these customers and you need to know how much is at stake. A spreadsheet is the perfect solution, both to make the calculations and to display your data.

Let me set up the hypothetical data in a new spreadsheet. Before we are through, we will use every trick covered so far.

Step One: Setting Up Our Data for 2004

In this sheet, we have listed our customers, created a centered heading (by merging the cells), and created row headers. Be sure to use the Copy feature for repeated items such as Widgets 1-5 and Per Item prices. Review Lesson 1 if any of this is difficult for you.

Step Two: Entering Formulas

There are lots of formulas to enter, but they are all old friends. The formula for Total Sales is Per Item cost times No. Sold, or D3 times C3 in the first instance. After you have input the first formula, save time by copying and pasting it into cells E4 through E7. As a better alternative, select cell E3, select the grab box in the lower right-hand corner of the cell, and drag it down to copy the formula into the other cells. Since you are using relative cell references, the formulas will all be correct. An even quicker way is to drag the formula down to the bottom of your worksheet (cell E35, for my sample sheet), then go back and delete the formula from the totals cells (E8, E15, E22, E29, and E35) and from the blank cells (E9, E16, E23, E30, and E35).

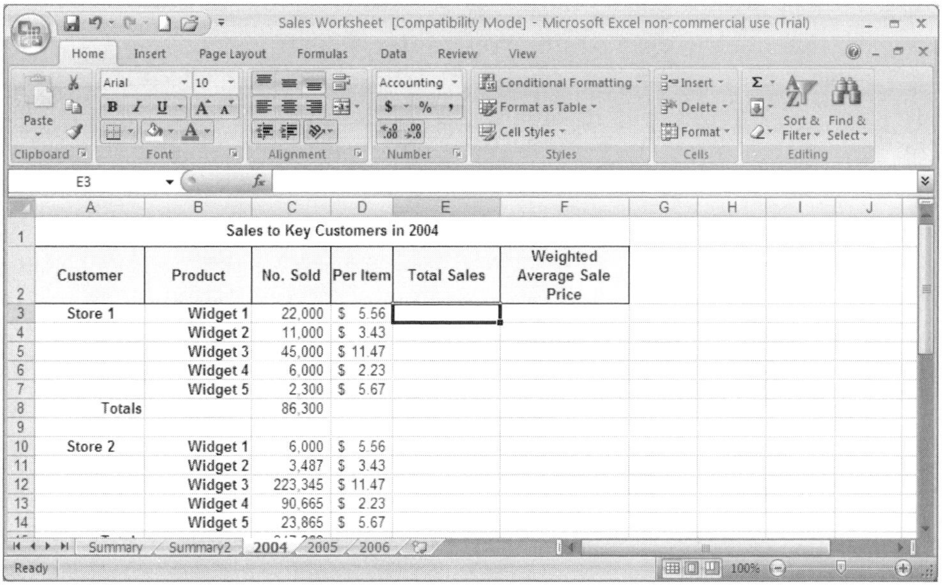

Figure 4-13: 2004 Sales Data

You can determine the totals (cells E8, E15, E22, E29, and E35) using the SUM function. Now we have calculated the number sold and the total amount of sales. Determining the Weighted Average Sale Price is equally simple. It is the total for Total Sales divided by the total for No. Sold.

Here are the results:

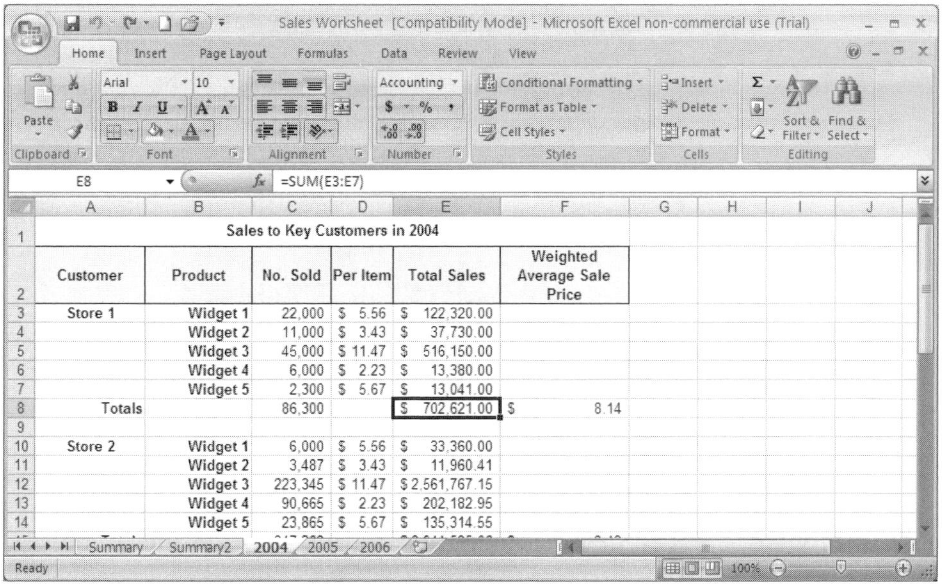

Figure 4-14: Completed 2004 Data

Step Three: Making the Other Worksheets

To make the other worksheets for this problem, start by copying your work for 2004 and pasting it into new worksheets for 2005 and 2006. (Block cells A1 through F36.) You will have to widen some of the columns to fit your data and you may want to adjust the first couple of rows for proper spacing. Or, you can right click on the worksheet tab and choose Move or Copy from the menu that appears. In the Move or Copy dialog box, select (move to end), then click the Create a copy checkbox. This process creates an exact duplicate worksheet with all the formatting intact. Either way, it beats re-keying your work.

Next, change the pricing data on your other two worksheets. (For this example, we are just making up numbers anyway.) Because your formulas are dynamic (they use cell references rather than hard numbers), all of your totals change appropriately.

Step Four: Making a Summary Spreadsheet

Now that you have input three years of hypothetical data, it is time to build a summary spreadsheet. While this step is not required, it makes it far simpler to comprehend your data. And, it is simple to do.

Let me show you my summary worksheet first. Then I will teach you how to create it.

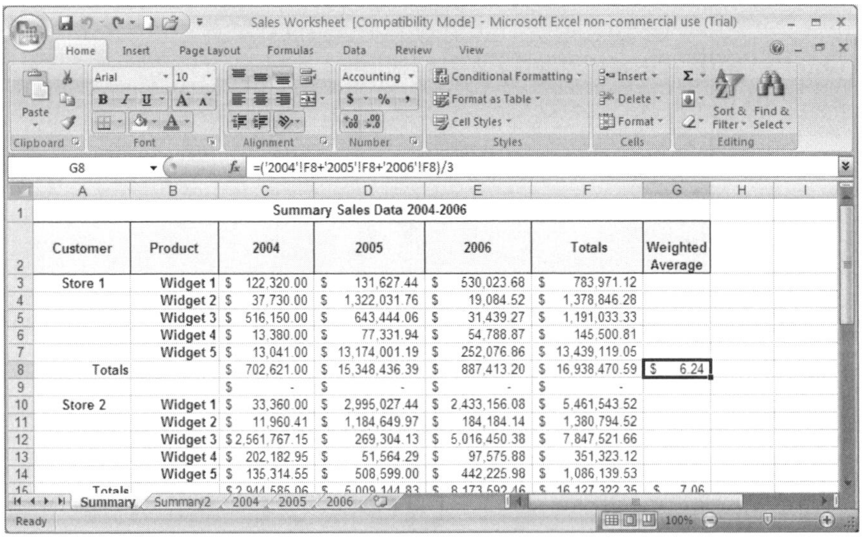

Figure 4-15: The Summary Sales Spreadsheet

Create or open a new worksheet (click on the Insert Worksheet tab to the right of the other worksheet tabs or choose the Insert menu under the Cells section of the Home menu and choose Insert Sheet) and name it "Summary." Next, create the column headers. They are similar to the column headings for the yearly worksheets but contain slightly different headings. Note that I have formatted the column headings by centering them horizontally and vertically, boldfacing the headings, and coloring and adding borders to the boxes. The company headings in columns A and B were copied from the other worksheets.

Now you have a worksheet that looks like this:

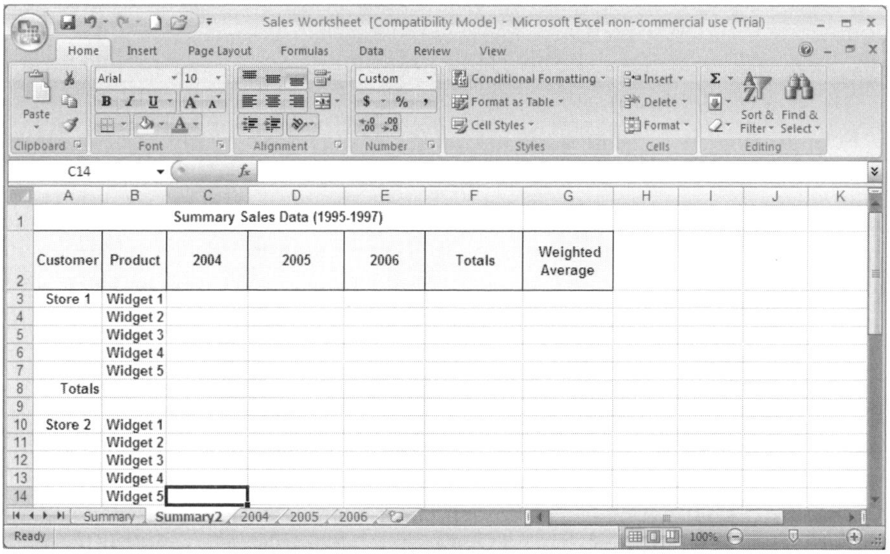

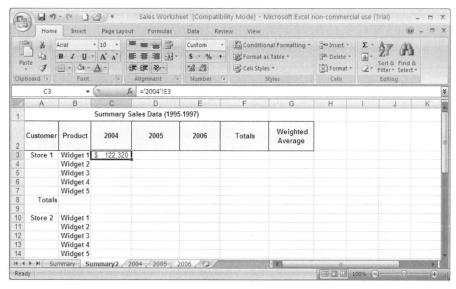

Figure 4-16: Setting Up the Summary

We are ready to insert the data. Rather than key any of the data, use cell references instead. Start with cell C3. Press the = key to execute a formula. Then click on the spreadsheet called 2004 and click on cell E3 (Total Sales for Widget 1 in 2004). Then press Enter. In cell C3 of the Summary sheet, Excel displays the value contained in cell E3.

In Excel terms, your formula is: ='2004'!E3. In practical terms, it is easier to click your way through this formula than to figure out how to enter it yourself.

Figure 4-17: Creating References to Other Pages

For the rest of the cells in this column, drag the formula from cell C3 downward to the end of your worksheet. Excel inputs the proper numbers (the relative cells) from the 2004 worksheet. (You may need to clean up the blank cells. Simply delete the formula.) Suddenly, you have entered a lot of data with very little work.

Repeat these steps for cells D3 (2005 data) and E3 (2006 data). By now, you should be able to do this in about 30 seconds.

We are on the home stretch. To calculate the totals, we need only sum the cells for the three years of data. Thus, cell F3 represents the sum of cells C3, D3, and E3. There are lots of ways to get there, but try this. Click on cell F3 and then click on the SUM button. Excel magically assumes you want to sum the three cells to the left—namely cells C3, D3, and E3, which is exactly right. Press Enter, and you have your correct sum.

You could repeat this step for each total down to cell F35. But it is much easier to drag the grab handle in cell F3 down to cell F35. It copies the correct SUM formula into each cell.

The last calculation is the weighted average sales price for each customer. We need to create a simple formula for this one. In other words, the formula is the sum of the weighted average sales price for Store 1 purchases in 2004, 2005, and 2006 divided by 3.

Here is how to create the formula with Excel:

1. Click on cell G8 on your summary page.
2. Press = to start your formula.
3. Type an open/left parenthesis (to begin the first part of the formula.
4. Click on your 2004 spreadsheet and then click on cell F8.
5. Press the + key.
6. Click on 2005 and select cell F8.
7. Press the + key.
8. Click on 2006 and select cell F8.
9. Type a closed/right parentheses) to complete the first part of the formula.
10. Type /3 (slash 3, which means divided by 3) and press Enter.

Your formula is complete and you have the weighted average for Store 1 over the three-year period. The Excel formula we have created looks like this:

=('2004'!F8+'2005'!F8+'2006'!F8)/3

To complete the weighted average calculations for the other customers, simply copy the formula in cell G8 and paste it into cells G15, G22, G29, and G36. When you paste the formula into these cells, Excel changes the cell references to match the proper cells for each of the other customers. Once again, the relative Cell References feature saves us a tremendous amount of time.

We have covered as much about formulas that you may ever need to know. If you combine this knowledge with what we have learned about setting up and formatting a spreadsheet, there is very little you cannot do. Let's test your knowledge in Lesson 5, where we will discuss how to create some practical business spreadsheets.

Business Spreadsheets

To this point, we have used litigation examples for our lessons. I am a litigator by trade, and I took these examples from my practice. Many of you are not litigators. You are real estate, or business, or trust and estates lawyers (or intellectual property, or government—or whatever). So how about a few non-litigation examples? Once you dive below the surface, they really are not much different than the ones we have already seen, but we can use them as a sort of a graduation exercise. At the least, I can get you non-litigators thinking about how to use spreadsheets in your own practice. And, we can all test out the concepts we have been working on in our first four lessons. So here we go with a few business spreadsheet examples.

Calculating Sales and Use Taxes

One of my former partners specializes in state sales and use tax issues. Recently, a client approached him about purchasing the assets of about thirty small businesses located throughout the Front Range (the eastern part of Colorado). The total purchase price was just under $2 million. He wondered about the state and local sales tax implications of his planned purchases.

Since the businesses were located in different cities and counties, my partner set up a spreadsheet to assist in determining how much tax would be owed. He started by setting up the following simple grid:

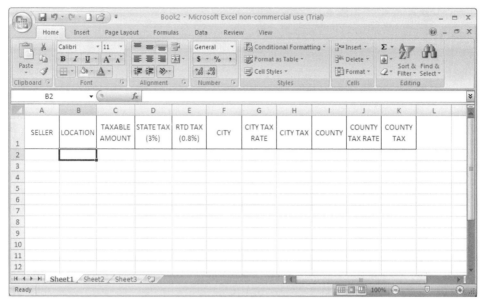

Figure 5-1: The Beginning Grid

As you can see, there are a number of governmental entities looking to take a bite out of this transaction. We have state sales taxes, Regional Transportation District (RTD) taxes, and city and county taxes.

The next step is to add the basic information regarding the purchaser, purchase price, and location of the facility. There is no easy way to do this unless you can find someone else to key it in.

	SELLER	LOCATION	TAXABLE AMOUNT	STATE TAX (3%)	RTD TAX (0.8%)	CITY	CITY TAX RATE	CITY TAX	COUNTY	COUNTY TAX RATE	COUNTY TAX
2											
3	Smith	111 Washington	$ 5,467.00								
4	Thomas	222 Adams	$123,589.00								
5	Greene	333 Jefferson	$ 58,679.00								
6	Benson	444 Madison	$ 3,476.00								
7	Jackson	555 Monroe	$ 56,444.00								
8	Brooke	66 Quincy Adam	$ 3,987.00								
9	Scott	777 Jackson	$ 55,678.00								
10	Stamper	81 Van Buren	$ 53,777.00								
11	Jones	992 Harrison	$ 20,056.00								
12	Wiley	1001 Tyler	$789,544.00								
13	Poe	1112 Polk	$ 34,999.00								
14	Poe	13 Taylor Way	$ 45,666.00								
15	Miller	14 Filmore	$ 12,333.00								
16	Miller	12 Pierce	$ 30,000.00								
17	Romberg	15 Buchanan	$ 40,000.00								
18	Abely	16 Lincoln	$ 90,888.00								
19	Pikachou	17 Johnson	$ 4,545.00								
20	Hembrough	18 Grant Ave	$ 78,999.00								

Figure 5-2: The Basic Data

Our state sales tax is 3 percent. To determine the state's share of this transaction, we simple multiply the taxable amount by .03. Using our point and click method, we can determine that the tax owed for the purchase of the first facility is C3 times .03. This formula is entered into cell D3.

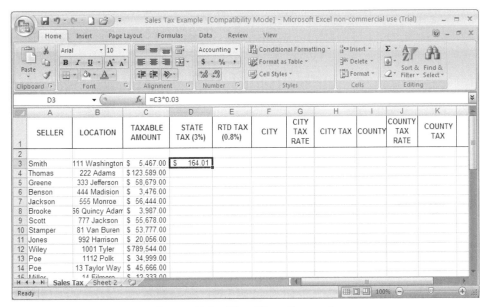

Figure 5-3: The First Formula

From here, it is a simple matter to drag down our formula from cell D3 to cell D32 (not visible in this screen capture). Like this:

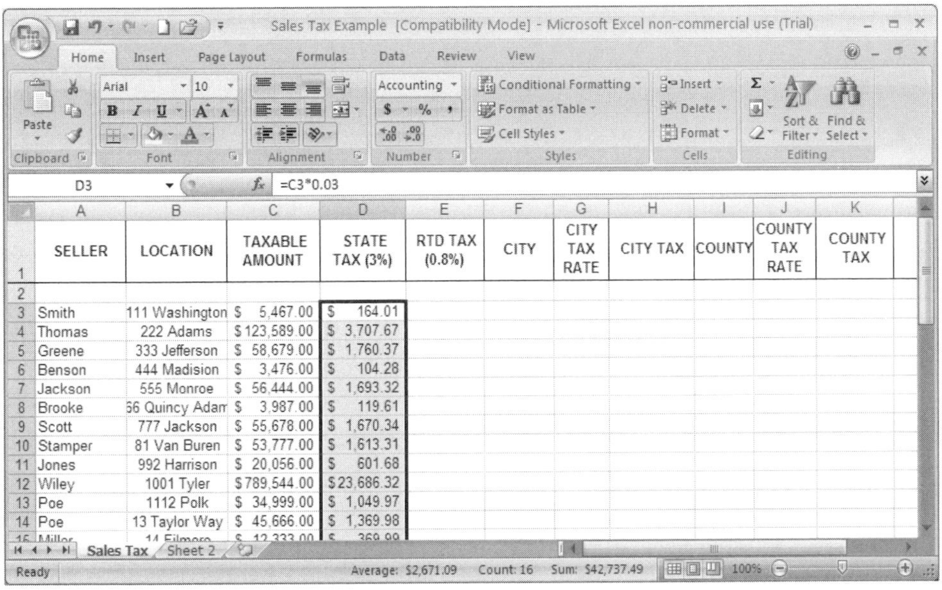

Figure 5-4: Dragging Down the Formula

Let's make quick work of the rest of the columns. RTD tax is .8 percent or .008. The formula for cell E3 is D3*.008. You can drag that formula down the column just as you did for column D. Here is the result:

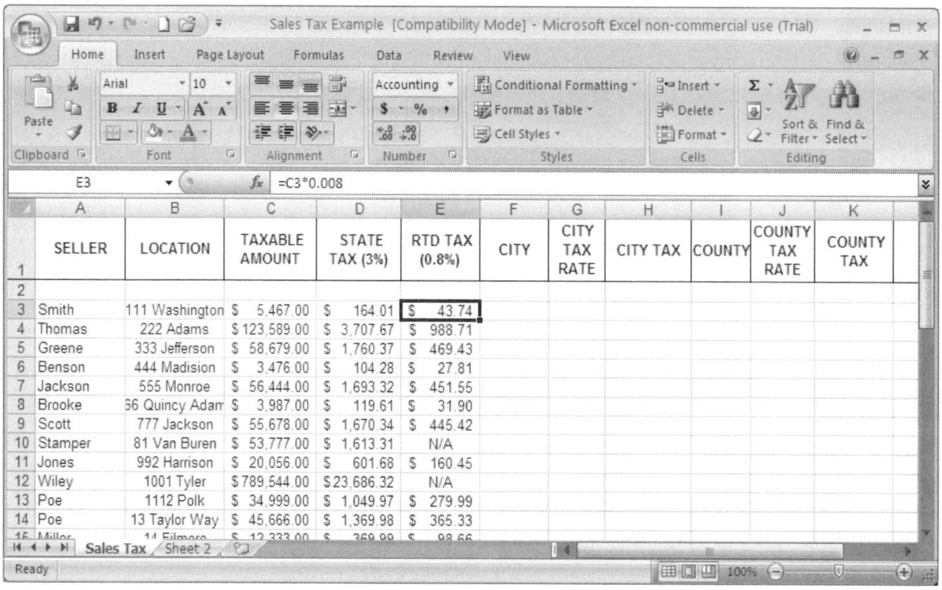

	SELLER	LOCATION	TAXABLE AMOUNT	STATE TAX (3%)	RTD TAX (0.8%)	CITY	CITY TAX RATE	CITY TAX	COUNTY	COUNTY TAX RATE	COUNTY TAX
3	Smith	111 Washington	$ 5,467.00	$ 164.01	$ 43.74						
4	Thomas	222 Adams	$ 123,589.00	$ 3,707.67	$ 988.71						
5	Greene	333 Jefferson	$ 58,679.00	$ 1,760.37	$ 469.43						
6	Benson	444 Madision	$ 3,476.00	$ 104.28	$ 27.81						
7	Jackson	555 Monroe	$ 56,444.00	$ 1,693.32	$ 451.55						
8	Brooke	56 Quincy Adam	$ 3,987.00	$ 119.61	$ 31.90						
9	Scott	777 Jackson	$ 55,678.00	$ 1,670.34	$ 445.42						
10	Stamper	81 Van Buren	$ 53,777.00	$ 1,613.31	N/A						
11	Jones	992 Harrison	$ 20,056.00	$ 601.68	$ 160.45						
12	Wiley	1001 Tyler	$ 789,544.00	$ 23,686.32	N/A						
13	Poe	1112 Polk	$ 34,999.00	$ 1,049.97	$ 279.99						
14	Poe	13 Taylor Way	$ 45,666.00	$ 1,369.98	$ 365.33						

Figure 5-5: Adding the RTD Tax

Where did the "N/A" come from? Not all of the businesses were in the RTD district, so we went back and added "N/A" to those rows that were outside the district.

After we key in the proper city, county, and city and county tax rates, we can fill in the rest of the columns using the same simple formulas.

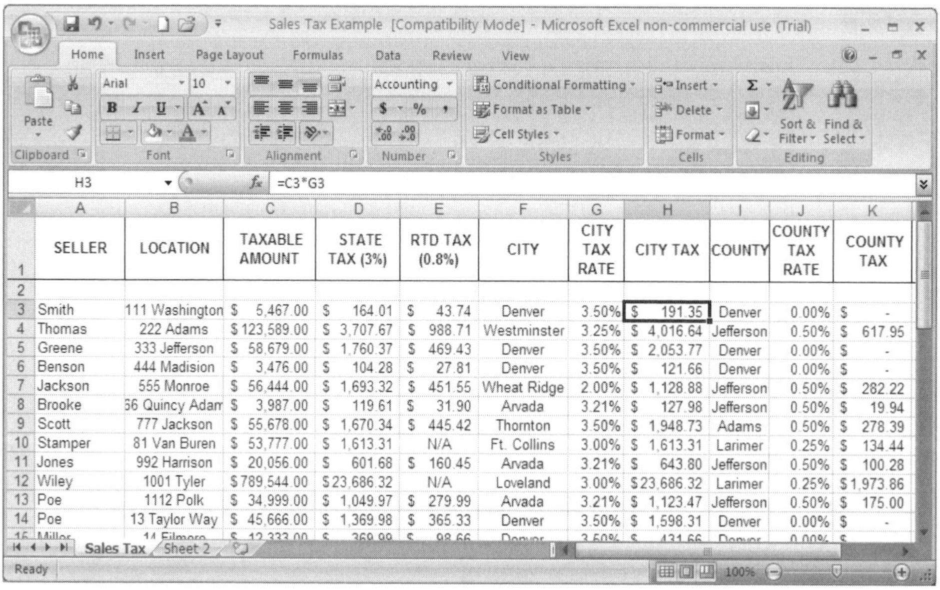

	SELLER	LOCATION	TAXABLE AMOUNT	STATE TAX (3%)	RTD TAX (0.8%)	CITY	CITY TAX RATE	CITY TAX	COUNTY	COUNTY TAX RATE	COUNTY TAX
3	Smith	111 Washington	$ 5,467.00	$ 164.01	$ 43.74	Denver	3.50%	$ 191.35	Denver	0.00%	$ -
4	Thomas	222 Adams	$ 123,589.00	$ 3,707.67	$ 988.71	Westminster	3.25%	$ 4,016.64	Jefferson	0.50%	$ 617.95
5	Greene	333 Jefferson	$ 58,679.00	$ 1,760.37	$ 469.43	Denver	3.50%	$ 2,053.77	Denver	0.00%	$ -
6	Benson	444 Madision	$ 3,476.00	$ 104.28	$ 27.81	Denver	3.50%	$ 121.66	Denver	0.00%	$ -
7	Jackson	555 Monroe	$ 56,444.00	$ 1,693.32	$ 451.55	Wheat Ridge	2.00%	$ 1,128.88	Jefferson	0.50%	$ 282.22
8	Brooke	56 Quincy Adam	$ 3,987.00	$ 119.61	$ 31.90	Arvada	3.21%	$ 127.98	Jefferson	0.50%	$ 19.94
9	Scott	777 Jackson	$ 55,678.00	$ 1,670.34	$ 445.42	Thornton	3.50%	$ 1,948.73	Adams	0.50%	$ 278.39
10	Stamper	81 Van Buren	$ 53,777.00	$ 1,613.31	N/A	Ft. Collins	3.00%	$ 1,613.31	Larimer	0.25%	$ 134.44
11	Jones	992 Harrison	$ 20,056.00	$ 601.68	$ 160.45	Arvada	3.21%	$ 643.80	Jefferson	0.50%	$ 100.28
12	Wiley	1001 Tyler	$ 789,544.00	$ 23,686.32	N/A	Loveland	3.00%	$ 23,686.32	Larimer	0.25%	$ 1,973.86
13	Poe	1112 Polk	$ 34,999.00	$ 1,049.97	$ 279.99	Arvada	3.21%	$ 1,123.47	Jefferson	0.50%	$ 175.00
14	Poe	13 Taylor Way	$ 45,666.00	$ 1,369.98	$ 365.33	Denver	3.50%	$ 1,598.31	Denver	0.00%	$ -

Figure 5-6: The Completed City/County/State Tax Spreadsheet

The final step is to calculate the sum of all the taxes being charged. We need to go to the bottom of the spreadsheet and use the SUM function command. (Consider freezing the panes before you do so to keep the headings visible. Click on cell A2 and then choose Window>Freeze Panes.)

Move to cell D34 and execute the SUM command, either by clicking on the AutoSum button on the toolbar or using the Formula command.

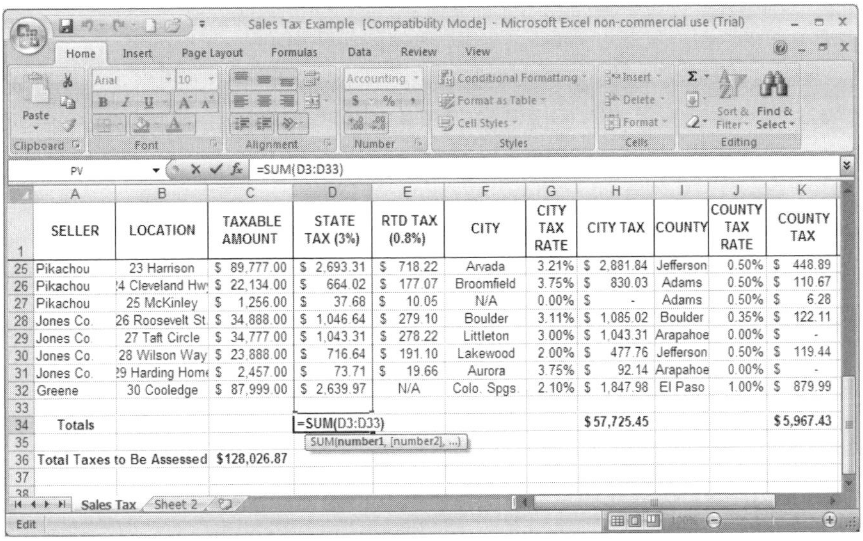

	SELLER	LOCATION	TAXABLE AMOUNT	STATE TAX (3%)	RTD TAX (0.8%)	CITY	CITY TAX RATE	CITY TAX	COUNTY	COUNTY TAX RATE	COUNTY TAX
25	Pikachou	23 Harrison	$ 89,777.00	$ 2,693.31	$ 718.22	Arvada	3.21%	$ 2,881.84	Jefferson	0.50%	$ 448.89
26	Pikachou	!4 Cleveland Hw	$ 22,134.00	$ 664.02	$ 177.07	Broomfield	3.75%	$ 830.03	Adams	0.50%	$ 110.67
27	Pikachou	25 McKinley	$ 1,256.00	$ 37.68	$ 10.05	N/A	0.00%	$ -	Adams	0.50%	$ 6.28
28	Jones Co.	26 Roosevelt St.	$ 34,888.00	$ 1,046.64	$ 279.10	Boulder	3.11%	$ 1,085.02	Boulder	0.35%	$ 122.11
29	Jones Co.	27 Taft Circle	$ 34,777.00	$ 1,043.31	$ 278.22	Littleton	3.00%	$ 1,043.31	Arapahoe	0.00%	$ -
30	Jones Co.	28 Wilson Way	$ 23,888.00	$ 716.64	$ 191.10	Lakewood	2.00%	$ 477.76	Jefferson	0.50%	$ 119.44
31	Jones Co.	!9 Harding Hom	$ 2,457.00	$ 73.71	$ 19.66	Aurora	3.75%	$ 92.14	Arapahoe	0.00%	$ -
32	Greene	30 Cooledge	$ 87,999.00	$ 2,639.97	N/A	Colo. Spgs.	2.10%	$ 1,847.98	El Paso	1.00%	$ 879.99
33											
34	Totals			=SUM(D3:D33)				$57,725.45			$5,967.43
35											
36	Total Taxes to Be Assessed		$128,026.87								

Figure 5-7: Using the AutoSum Button

We can do the same with the other tax columns and then create a simple formula for the total for all the taxes likely to be assessed.

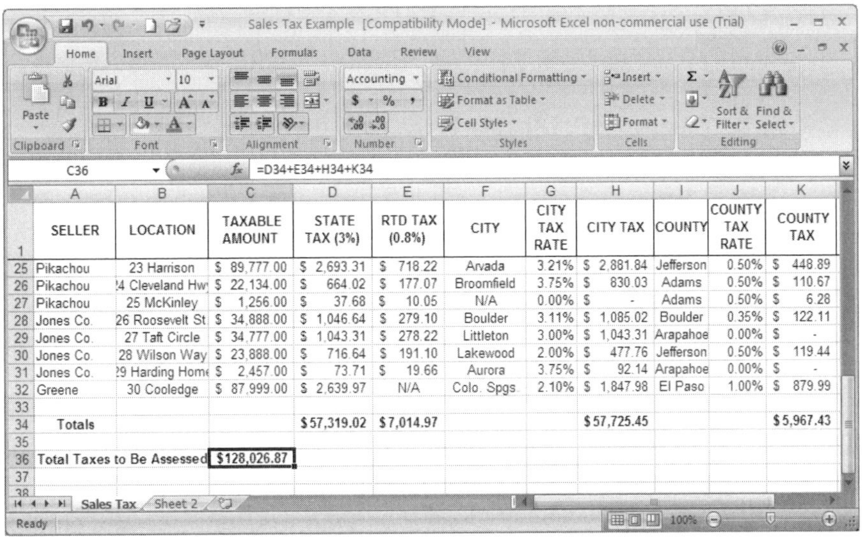

	SELLER	LOCATION	TAXABLE AMOUNT	STATE TAX (3%)	RTD TAX (0.8%)	CITY	CITY TAX RATE	CITY TAX	COUNTY	COUNTY TAX RATE	COUNTY TAX
25	Pikachou	23 Harrison	$ 89,777.00	$ 2,693.31	$ 718.22	Arvada	3.21%	$ 2,881.84	Jefferson	0.50%	$ 448.89
26	Pikachou	!4 Cleveland Hw	$ 22,134.00	$ 664.02	$ 177.07	Broomfield	3.75%	$ 830.03	Adams	0.50%	$ 110.67
27	Pikachou	25 McKinley	$ 1,256.00	$ 37.68	$ 10.05	N/A	0.00%	$ -	Adams	0.50%	$ 6.28
28	Jones Co.	26 Roosevelt St	$ 34,888.00	$ 1,046.64	$ 279.10	Boulder	3.11%	$ 1,085.02	Boulder	0.35%	$ 122.11
29	Jones Co.	27 Taft Circle	$ 34,777.00	$ 1,043.31	$ 278.22	Littleton	3.00%	$ 1,043.31	Arapahoe	0.00%	$ -
30	Jones Co.	28 Wilson Way	$ 23,888.00	$ 716.64	$ 191.10	Lakewood	2.00%	$ 477.76	Jefferson	0.50%	$ 119.44
31	Jones Co.	!9 Harding Hom	$ 2,457.00	$ 73.71	$ 19.66	Aurora	3.75%	$ 92.14	Arapahoe	0.00%	$ -
32	Greene	30 Cooledge	$ 87,999.00	$ 2,639.97	N/A	Colo. Spgs.	2.10%	$ 1,847.98	El Paso	1.00%	$ 879.99
33											
34	Totals			$57,319.02	$7,014.97			$57,725.45			$5,967.43
35											
36	Total Taxes to Be Assessed		$128,026.87								

Figure 5-8: The Final Calculations

We have finished our spreadsheet and have our answer.

A Property Tax Calculator

One of our clients planned to buy a pipeline consisting of about 275 miles of gas pipe in another state. The pipeline runs through fifteen counties. We knew that each county would assess property taxes on the pipeline and compressor stations. How much annual property tax would be due on the pipeline?

We will set up a simple spreadsheet to calculate and total the taxes owed to each county. Let's start with a simple grid. Use your formatting options to wrap, boldface, and center the headings. Use the border options to set off the headings from the rest of the spreadsheet.

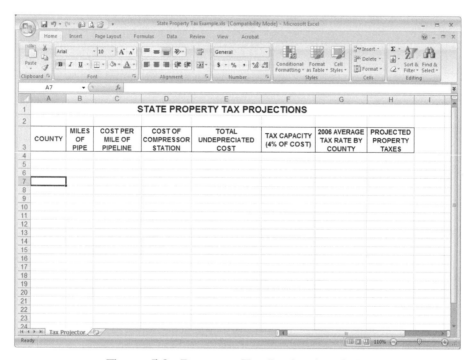

Figure 5-9: Property Tax Projection Grid

Next, key in the basic data as shown in Figure 5-10. Since the cost per mile of pipeline stays the same throughout, you can copy that value from row to row (drag the value in cell C4 to the bottom of the list). Or, in cell C5, create the formula =C4 and then drag it down to the bottom of your spreadsheet. That way, if you change the value in cell C4, it changes for the other cells in that column.

From here, we need to fill in the formulas for the rest of the spreadsheet. Start with column E, which is labeled "Total Undepreciated Cost." The formula for cell E4 is =(B4*C4)+D4. In other words, we multiply the miles of pipeline times the undepreciated cost per mile of pipeline. Then we add that amount to the cost of a compressor station, if any. This gives us the "Total Undepreciated Cost" for our first row, as shown in Figure 5-11.

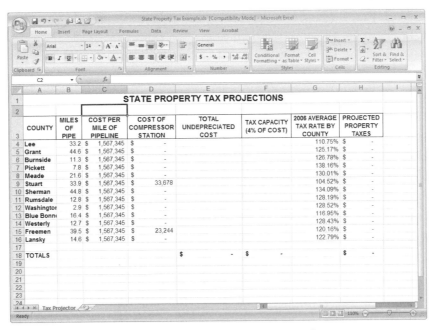

Figure 5-10: The Basic Information

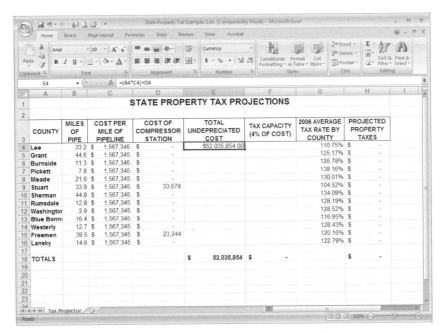

Figure 5-11: Total Undepreciated Cost

The next step is to drag the formula down to row 16. Click on cell E4 and drag the grab handle to the bottom of your spreadsheet. The formula fills in using relative cell references.

Now determine the tax capacity for each county. This is based on 4 percent of undepreciated cost. For cell F4, the formula is =E4*.04. Drag that formula down to the bottom of your spreadsheet as well. Lastly, calculate the projected property taxes by multiplying cell F4 times cell G4. When we drag down that column, the results should look like this:

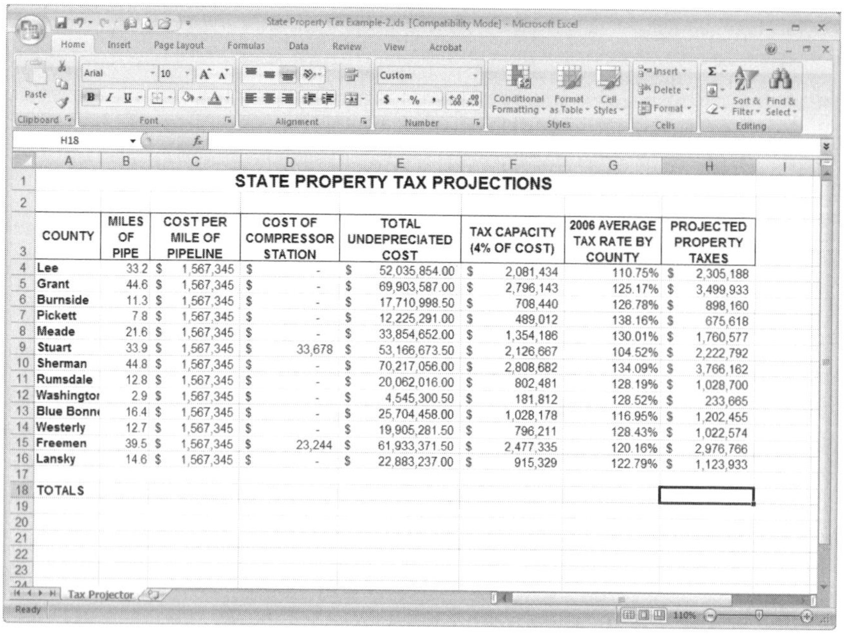

STATE PROPERTY TAX PROJECTIONS

COUNTY	MILES OF PIPE	COST PER MILE OF PIPELINE	COST OF COMPRESSOR STATION	TOTAL UNDEPRECIATED COST	TAX CAPACITY (4% OF COST)	2006 AVERAGE TAX RATE BY COUNTY	PROJECTED PROPERTY TAXES
Lee	33.2	$ 1,567,345	$ -	$ 52,035,854.00	$ 2,081,434	110.75%	$ 2,305,188
Grant	44.6	$ 1,567,345	$ -	$ 69,903,587.00	$ 2,796,143	125.17%	$ 3,499,933
Burnside	11.3	$ 1,567,345	$ -	$ 17,710,998.50	$ 708,440	126.78%	$ 898,160
Pickett	7.8	$ 1,567,345	$ -	$ 12,225,291.00	$ 489,012	138.16%	$ 675,618
Meade	21.6	$ 1,567,345	$ -	$ 33,854,652.00	$ 1,354,186	130.01%	$ 1,760,577
Stuart	33.9	$ 1,567,345	$ 33,678	$ 53,166,673.50	$ 2,126,667	104.52%	$ 2,222,792
Sherman	44.8	$ 1,567,345	$ -	$ 70,217,056.00	$ 2,808,682	134.09%	$ 3,766,162
Rumsdale	12.8	$ 1,567,345	$ -	$ 20,062,016.00	$ 802,481	128.19%	$ 1,028,700
Washingtoı	2.9	$ 1,567,345	$ -	$ 4,545,300.50	$ 181,812	128.52%	$ 233,665
Blue Bonn	16.4	$ 1,567,345	$ -	$ 25,704,458.00	$ 1,028,178	116.95%	$ 1,202,455
Westerly	12.7	$ 1,567,345	$ -	$ 19,905,281.50	$ 796,211	128.43%	$ 1,022,574
Freemen	39.5	$ 1,567,345	$ 23,244	$ 61,933,371.50	$ 2,477,335	120.16%	$ 2,976,766
Lansky	14.6	$ 1,567,345	$ -	$ 22,883,237.00	$ 915,329	122.79%	$ 1,123,933
TOTALS							

Figure 5-12: Adding Formulas

All we have left to do is calculate and add totals. Use the SUM function key on the toolbar or the SUM function formula from the Formula bar.

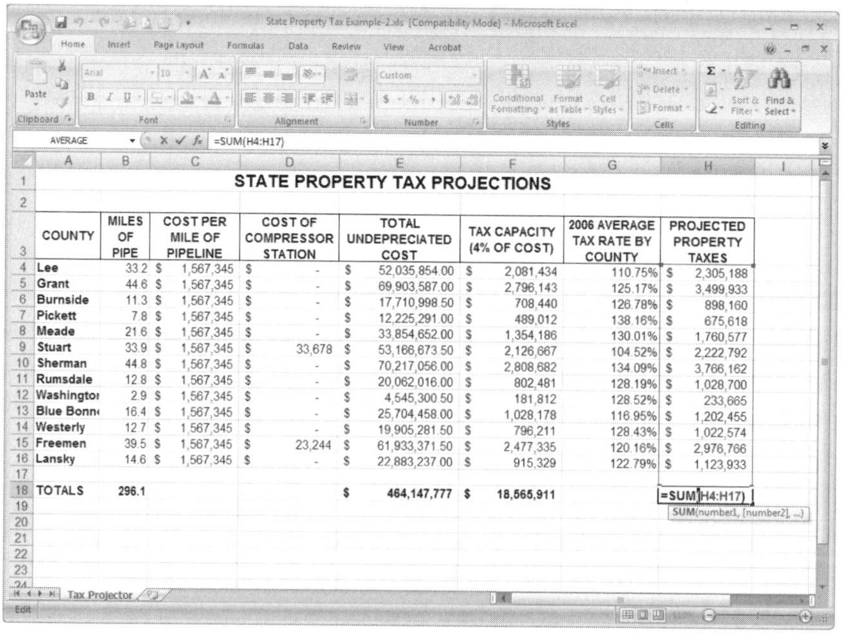

=SUM(H4:H17)

STATE PROPERTY TAX PROJECTIONS

COUNTY	MILES OF PIPE	COST PER MILE OF PIPELINE	COST OF COMPRESSOR STATION	TOTAL UNDEPRECIATED COST	TAX CAPACITY (4% OF COST)	2006 AVERAGE TAX RATE BY COUNTY	PROJECTED PROPERTY TAXES
Lee	33.2	$ 1,567,345	$ -	$ 52,035,854.00	$ 2,081,434	110.75%	$ 2,305,188
Grant	44.6	$ 1,567,345	$ -	$ 69,903,587.00	$ 2,796,143	125.17%	$ 3,499,933
Burnside	11.3	$ 1,567,345	$ -	$ 17,710,998.50	$ 708,440	126.78%	$ 898,160
Pickett	7.8	$ 1,567,345	$ -	$ 12,225,291.00	$ 489,012	138.16%	$ 675,618
Meade	21.6	$ 1,567,345	$ -	$ 33,854,652.00	$ 1,354,186	130.01%	$ 1,760,577
Stuart	33.9	$ 1,567,345	$ 33,678	$ 53,166,673.50	$ 2,126,667	104.52%	$ 2,222,792
Sherman	44.8	$ 1,567,345	$ -	$ 70,217,056.00	$ 2,808,682	134.09%	$ 3,766,162
Rumsdale	12.8	$ 1,567,345	$ -	$ 20,062,016.00	$ 802,481	128.19%	$ 1,028,700
Washingtoı	2.9	$ 1,567,345	$ -	$ 4,545,300.50	$ 181,812	128.52%	$ 233,665
Blue Bonn	16.4	$ 1,567,345	$ -	$ 25,704,458.00	$ 1,028,178	116.95%	$ 1,202,455
Westerly	12.7	$ 1,567,345	$ -	$ 19,905,281.50	$ 796,211	128.43%	$ 1,022,574
Freemen	39.5	$ 1,567,345	$ 23,244	$ 61,933,371.50	$ 2,477,335	120.16%	$ 2,976,766
Lansky	14.6	$ 1,567,345	$ -	$ 22,883,237.00	$ 915,329	122.79%	$ 1,123,933
TOTALS	296.1			$ 464,147,777	$ 18,565,911		=SUM(H4:H17)

Figure 5-13: Totaling the Projection Spreadsheet

You Have More Income!

One of our business clients came to us with a problem we would all like to have. A partnership was threatening to distribute more income to him than he had originally anticipated. He wondered what impact this might have on his taxes, particularly as it related to itemized deductions and personal exemptions (which phase out in a Byzantine fashion after your income reaches a certain level).

We prepared a simple two-page spreadsheet to determine how the extra income might impact these deductions. Here is how the first page, which projects income taxes for 2006, looks:

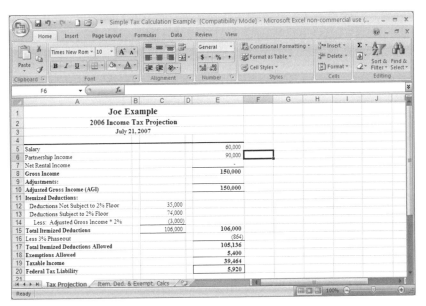

Figure 5-14: Income Tax Projection

Most of the information here is straightforward and will be easy reading for tax and estates lawyers. The layout, formatting, and most of the formulas should now be simple as well.

Figures for salary and partnership income were provided by the client. The total gross income figure is simply the sum of the cells E5, E6 and E7: =SUM(E5:E7). Adjusted gross income is simply the difference between cells E8 and E9 (in this case there is no difference).

The key question here was what impact would the extra income have on itemized deductions and exemptions. To find out, we need to make three separate calculations.

First, we must determine whether the extra income impacts itemized deductions. To do so, we calculate the effect of the extra income on Joe's miscellaneous itemized deductions. An individual is allowed to deduct miscellaneous itemized deductions to the extent that the deductions exceed 2 percent of his adjusted gross income. Using that formula, we multiply Joe's AGI by 2 percent. The result, $3,000, is displayed as a negative number in cell C14 in Figure 5-14 on page 61.

The sum of Joe's itemized deductions not subject to the 2 percent floor (C12), his itemized deductions subject to the 2 percent floor (C13), and the 2 percent of AGI phase-out amount (C14) is calculated in cell C15, and then, for purposes of further calculations, carried through a simple = formula to cell E15 on a second spreadsheet labeled "Item. Ded. & Exempt."

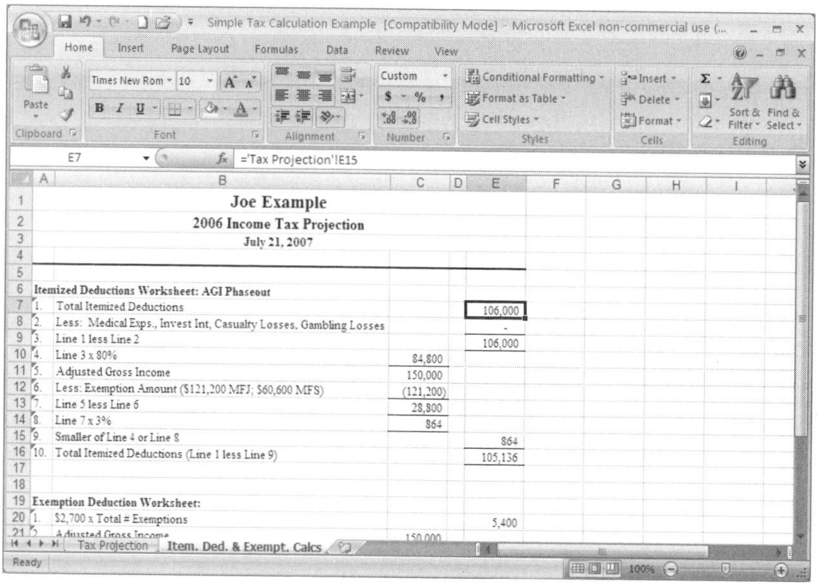

Figure 5-15: Itemized Deductions and Exemptions Calculator

Our second calculation is to determine the effect of the additional income on Joe's total allowable itemized deductions. This requires two sub-calculations. First, we calculate 80 percent of Joe's total itemized deductions. The resulting number in this case is $84,800 as shown in cell C10. Then we determine the difference between adjusted gross income and the exemption amount ($121,200, in this case, for a married couple filing jointly). Per the tax formula, we take 3 percent of that amount and display the result, $864, in cell C14.

We then compare the amount in cell C14 with the amount in cell C10. Since $864 is less than $84,800, we use $864 as our phase-out number. This amount is entered as a negative number in cell E16 on our first spreadsheet.

The total itemized deductions allowed is then calculated in cell E17 of our first spreadsheet by adding the total itemized deductions in cell E15 to the 3 percent of AGI phase out, which was carried to cell E16. We finally have an answer to part of our esoteric question. Joe's itemized deductions are reduced in total by $3,864 and, therefore, will be affected by the increased partnership income he may receive.

Sidebar: Linking Cells

Notice that the formula for cell C7 is linked to cell E15 on the preceding spreadsheet. By linking cells in different spreadsheets, you can ensure that all of the calculations are updated if your projections change. In this case, for example, if you learned that itemized deductions not subject to the 2 percent floor increased to $40,000, and you keyed that change into cell C12 of the Tax Projection spreadsheet, your entire spreadsheet would recalculate, including the number used in cell E7 on the second spreadsheet. This ability to link cells, whether to another cell on the same spreadsheet, another cell on a different spreadsheet in the same workbook, or another cell in an entirely different workbook file is a big reason why this software is so useful for "what if?" calculations.

Step 9 of the itemized deduction calculation requires us to use the lesser of cells C10 or C14 and display that result in cell E15. To work this small bit of magic automatically, we need an additional lesson in programming. Here is the formula we used:

=IF(C10<C14, C10, C14)

Programmers call these IF statements. It tells the computer to take one action if a condition is met, and to take another, if it is not met. This kind of programming is beyond the scope of this book, but this particular statement is not too difficult to decipher, and you can modify it to fit lots of similar situations. Here it is in English: If the amount in cell C10 is less than the amount in cell C14, then insert that amount in cell E15. If it is not less, then insert the amount of cell C14 in cell E15.

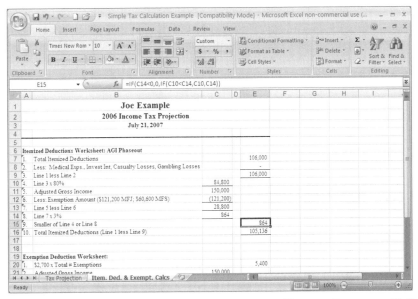

Figure 5-16: Programming IF Statements to Choose Between Cells

In Excel language, the syntax works this way:

=IF(	This tells Excel to create a formula using an IF, THEN, ELSE condition. The parentheses group the elements of the formula.
C10<C14,	The first element of the formula is the condition to evaluate. In this case, we want to know if the value in C10 is less than the value in C14. The comma is required to separate the elements.
C10,	The next element tells Excel what to do if the condition is met (that is, if the condition is true). Here, we tell Excel that if the condition is met, THEN use the value of cell C10 here.
C14)	This is the third element of the formula, the ELSE condition. We tell Excel what to do if our original condition is not met. Here we tell Excel to insert the value of cell C14 as our result. The closing parenthesis is required to end the IF statement.

Make sense? You can craft IF statements any time you need to by using this relatively simple formula.

There is a similar IF statement in the exemption calculation. Each exemption is worth $2,700. The exemption phase out requires a comparison between adjusted gross income and a threshold amount, which varies depending on the status of the filer. If the difference between cell C21 (adjusted gross income) and cell C22 (the exemption amount) is less than zero, there is no impact on the phase out. But, if Joe's income had increased by a larger amount, say $180,000, there would be an impact. Here is the result of a change in Joe's partnership income to $180,000:

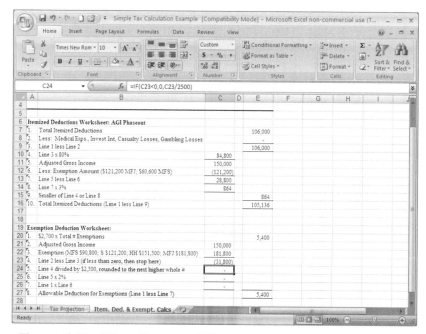

Figure 5-17: What Happens If Partnership Income Increases?

As you can see, the exemption amount would drop from $5,400 to $2,886. Total itemized deductions would drop from $105,636 to $100,636. With a properly built spreadsheet, we can do as many "what if" calculations as we like.

Before I close out this section, let me point out the second IF statement in this spreadsheet. If the result in step four of our exemption calculation is less than zero, there is no impact on the exemption and no need for further calculations. If it is greater, further calculations, steps 5, 6, and 7, are required. Thus, we use an IF statement in cell C24. Here it is: =IF(C23<0,0,C23/2500). We have simply told Excel to determine whether the result in cell C23 is less than zero. If so, enter 0 in cell C24. If not, then divide the amount in cell C23 by 2500 and enter that result in cell C24. Make sense? These IF statements can be mastered—even by us lawyers—once you get over the initial fear of programming.

Stock Ownership Disclosure

The client was a consolidator who specialized in combining smaller companies into a larger one and financing the whole thing through an initial public offering. Under the securities laws, a number of disclosures must be made, including full detail regarding stock ownership before and after the offering. With lots of companies being consolidated, tracking past stock ownership is a bit tricky. The situation is greatly compounded however, when post IPO ownership percentages vary greatly depending on how much stock is issued and what its offering price is. Since these decisions are often made at the last minute, just as the offering prospectus is going to press, we need spreadsheets to keep track of all this data.

We begin with a simple spreadsheet to track the acquisition prices for the various companies being acquired.

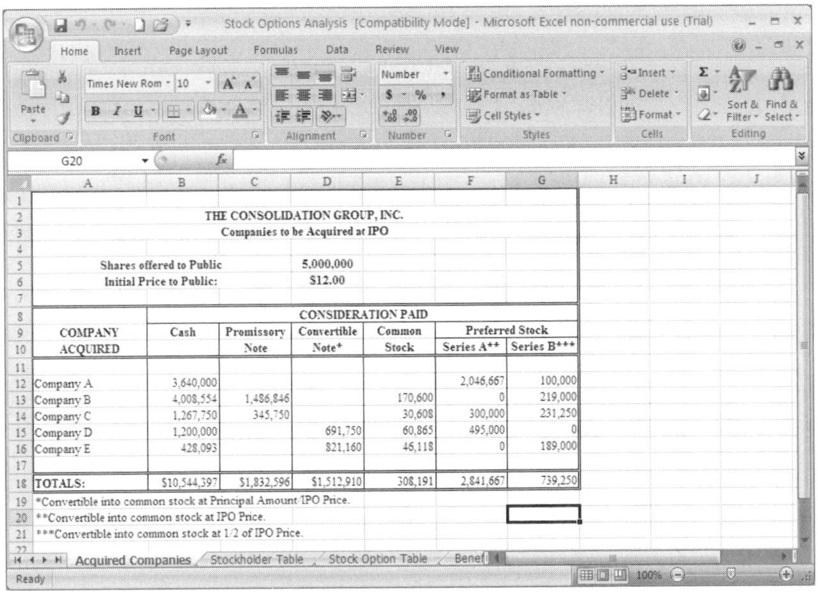

Figure 5-18: The Acquisition Spreadsheet

Most of this data represents information provided by the client. The totals are simply SUM functions. Note that cell D5 in Figure 5-18 contains the number of shares offered to the public and cell D6 is where you key in the initial offering price. Notice that these cells are linked to other pages in the spreadsheet and a change to either cell causes the spreadsheet to recalculate.

The next spreadsheet (Figure 5-19) tracks stock holdings. Most of this information was received from the client as well.

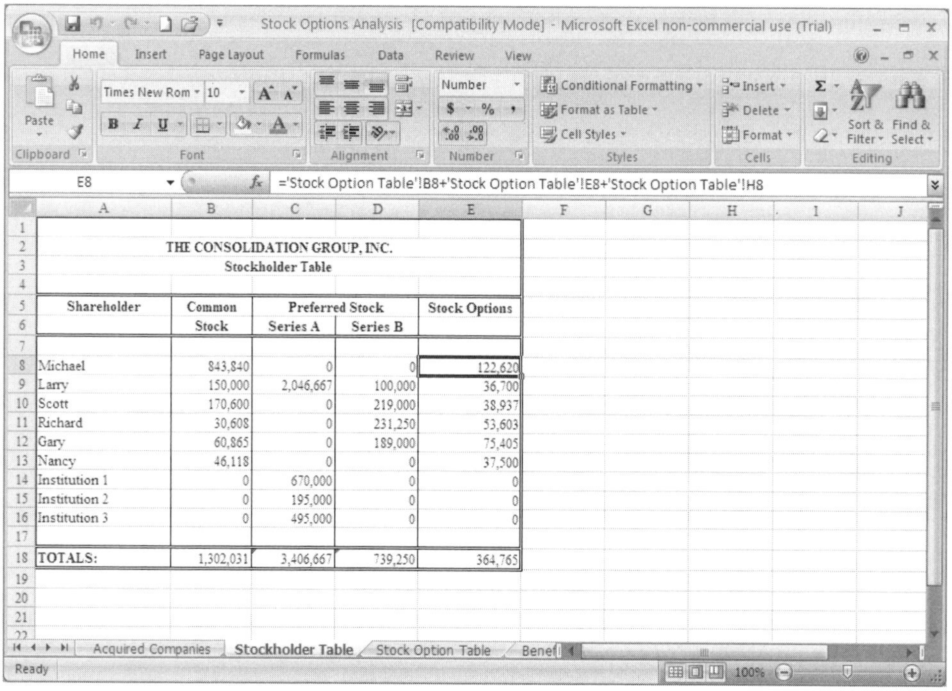

THE CONSOLIDATION GROUP, INC.
Stockholder Table

Shareholder	Common Stock	Preferred Stock Series A	Preferred Stock Series B	Stock Options
Michael	843,840	0	0	122,620
Larry	150,000	2,046,667	100,000	36,700
Scott	170,600	0	219,000	38,937
Richard	30,608	0	231,250	53,603
Gary	60,865	0	189,000	75,405
Nancy	46,118	0	0	37,500
Institution 1	0	670,000	0	0
Institution 2	0	195,000	0	0
Institution 3	0	495,000	0	0
TOTALS:	1,302,031	3,406,667	739,250	364,765

Figure 5-19: The Stockholder Table

Column E contains linked information. The number of options each shareholder receives is determined on a third spreadsheet (Figure 5-20), which tracks stock options. It represents the sum of three things: (1) the number of acquisition options; (2) the number of options received as part of the IPO; and (3) a number of incentive options also received as part of the IPO.

It is handy to use a separate spreadsheet to determine the total options received by each shareholder, because the value of those options is a function of the initial stock-offering price. That is why in columns G and J, we have the option "Prices" linked to the initial spreadsheet. For example, the formula for cell J8 is:

='Acquired Companies'!$D$6*0.5

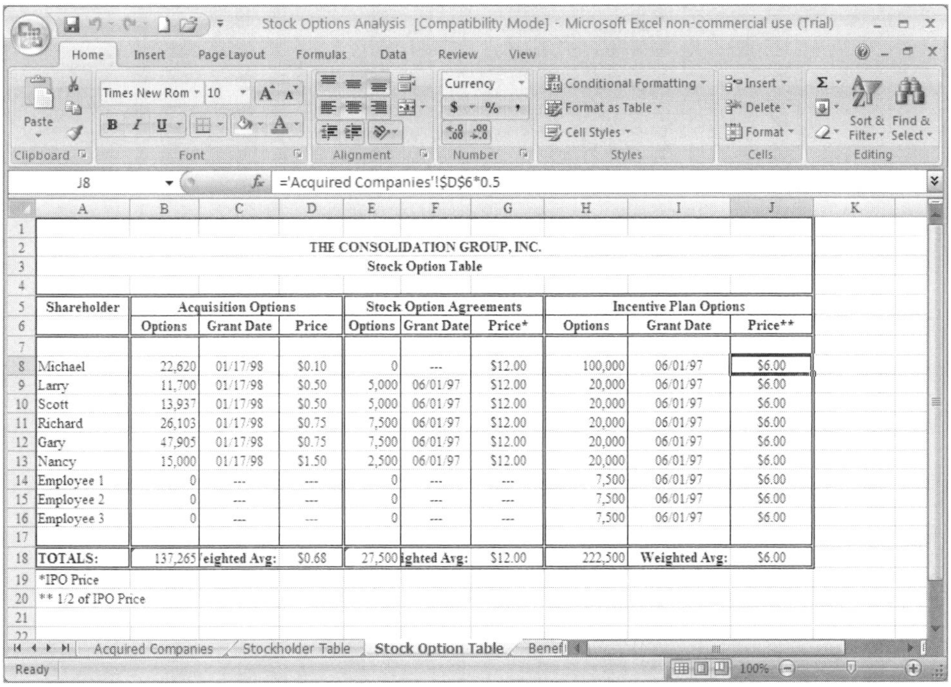

THE CONSOLIDATION GROUP, INC.
Stock Option Table

Shareholder	Acquisition Options			Stock Option Agreements			Incentive Plan Options		
	Options	Grant Date	Price	Options	Grant Date	Price*	Options	Grant Date	Price**
Michael	22,620	01/17/98	$0.10	0	---	$12.00	100,000	06/01/97	$6.00
Larry	11,700	01/17/98	$0.50	5,000	06/01/97	$12.00	20,000	06/01/97	$6.00
Scott	13,937	01/17/98	$0.50	5,000	06/01/97	$12.00	20,000	06/01/97	$6.00
Richard	26,103	01/17/98	$0.75	7,500	06/01/97	$12.00	20,000	06/01/97	$6.00
Gary	47,905	01/17/98	$0.75	7,500	06/01/97	$12.00	20,000	06/01/97	$6.00
Nancy	15,000	01/17/98	$1.50	2,500	06/01/97	$12.00	20,000	06/01/97	$6.00
Employee 1	0	---	---	0	---	---	7,500	06/01/97	$6.00
Employee 2	0	---	---	0	---	---	7,500	06/01/97	$6.00
Employee 3	0	---	---	0	---	---	7,500	06/01/97	$6.00
TOTALS:	137,265	'eighted Avg:	$0.68	27,500	ighted Avg:	$12.00	222,500	Weighted Avg:	$6.00

*IPO Price
** 1/2 of IPO Price

Figure 5-20: Stock Option Table

Translating to simple English, the formula says that the value of cell J8 is the value of cell D6 in the spreadsheet titled "Acquired Companies" times 0.5. As you may recall, we use $ signs in a formula such as this to ensure Excel knows that this cell reference should not change, even if we use the formula in additional rows (as we do in this spreadsheet). We want the formula in cells J9 through J16 to refer to cell D6 rather than cells D7 through D14. Refer back to my discussion on relative cell references in Lesson 3 if this is confusing to you.

All of this work leads to a final spreadsheet (Figure 5-21), which is designed to track beneficial ownership of the company both before and after the acquisition. Securities lawyers tell me this kind of information must be disclosed on the prospectus and that it can change right up to the last minute. We litigators know that if you are going to disclose it, you better have the math right. I trust a good spreadsheet better than hand calculations any day of the week.

So, let's work through the beneficial ownership spreadsheet in Figure 5-21:

We start with column B, which tracks common stock ownership. We take this information from the Stockholder Table spreadsheet. Note that the formula is relative. You can drag the formula for cell B8 downward and it picks up the appropriate information for Larry, Scott, Richard, etc.

The Consolidation Group, Inc. Beneficial Ownership Table spreadsheet. Formula bar shows B8 ='Stockholder Table'!B8

Beneficial Owner	Direct Common	Indirect Common	Convertible Common	Stock Options	Total Shares Beneficially Owned	Percentage Owned Pre-IPO	Post-IPO
Michael	843,840	55,833	0	122,620	899,673	69.10%	14.28%
Larry	150,000	0	187,222	36,700	337,222	22.64%	5.20%
Scott	170,600	0	36,500	38,937	207,100	15.47%	3.27%
Richard	30,608	0	38,542	53,603	69,150	5.16%	1.09%
Gary	60,865	0	89,146	75,405	150,011	10.78%	2.35%
Nancy	46,118	0	68,430	37,500	114,548	8.36%	1.80%
Institution 1	0	0	55,833	0	55,833	4.11%	0.88%
Institution 2	0	0	16,250	0	16,250	1.23%	0.26%
Institution 3	0	0	41,250	0	41,250	3.07%	0.65%
All directors and executive officers:					1,777,704	100.00%	26.23%
All shareholders, directors and exec					1,891,037	100.00%	27.44%

Figure 5-21: The Beneficial Ownership Spreadsheet

In this case, Michael is the only indirect stockowner. It turns out that he has an ownership interest in "Institution 1."

We need a column for "convertible common stock" because preferred shares will be converted to common stock as part of the IPO. Total shares of common stock for each Series A shareholder is determined by dividing the number of Series A preferred shares by the initial stock purchase price. For Series B shareholders, the formula is the number of shares divided by one-half of the initial purchase price.

Here is the Excel formula to make this calculation:

=('Stockholder Table'!C9/'Acquired Companies'!$D$6)+('Stockholder Table'!D9/(0.5*'Acquired Companies'!$D$6))

Reverting back to English, the formula is this: The number of shares of common stock Larry will receive is the sum of (1) his Series A stock (shown in cell C9 of the Stockholder spreadsheet) times the initial stock price (shown in cell D6 of the Acquired Companies spreadsheet) plus (2) the amount of his Series B stock times one-half of the initial stock price.

The calculation for total shares beneficially owned is simply the sum of the values in columns B, C, and D. For Michael, the formula is =B8+C8+D8.

Use the same formula for the rest of the shareholders.

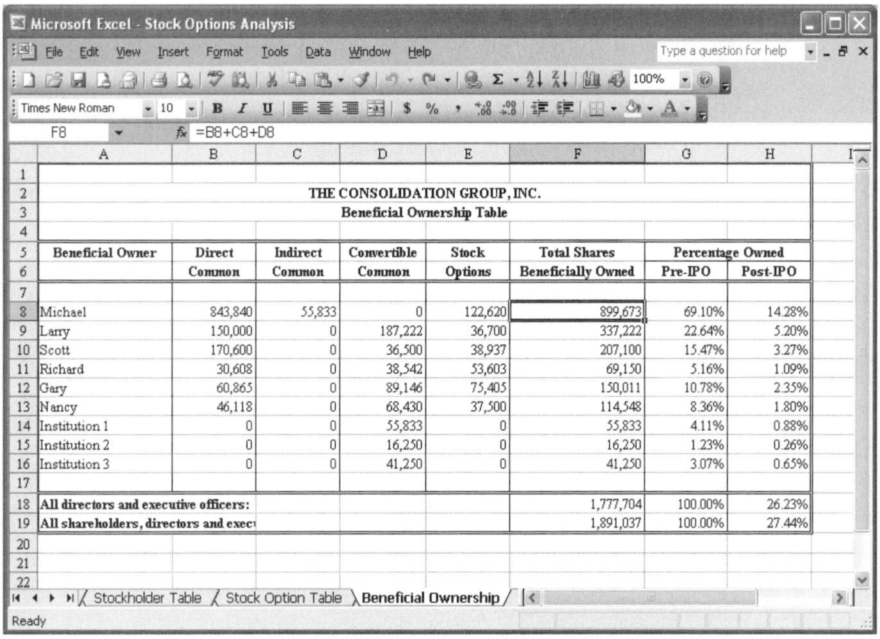

Figure 5-22: Total Shares Beneficially Owned

Our last two columns address shareholdings both before and after the public offering. Each requires reference to several other cells in the spreadsheets we have created and provides a good final example of complicated, but useful, formulas. I will show you how to determine the percentage of common stock the shareholders will own after the initial public offering. Here is the cell formula:

To determine Michael's percentage ownership of the company after the IPO, we need to divide the number of shares he beneficially owns by the total number of shares that will be outstanding. The Excel formula is this:

=F8/('Acquired Companies'!$D$5+'Stockholder Table'!$B$18+'Beneficial Ownership'!D8)

Cell F8 holds the total number of shares Michael owns. Cell D5 on the "Acquired Companies" spreadsheet contains the total number of shares to be offered to the public. Cell B18 on the "Stockholder Table" spreadsheet contains the total number of common stock owned prior to the IPO. Cell D8 on the "Beneficial Ownership" sheet contains the amount of convertible common stock Michael owns.

Thus, the formula is: total number of shares owned divided by total shares to be owned by the public and total shares owned by the original shareholders. The result is expressed as a percentage.

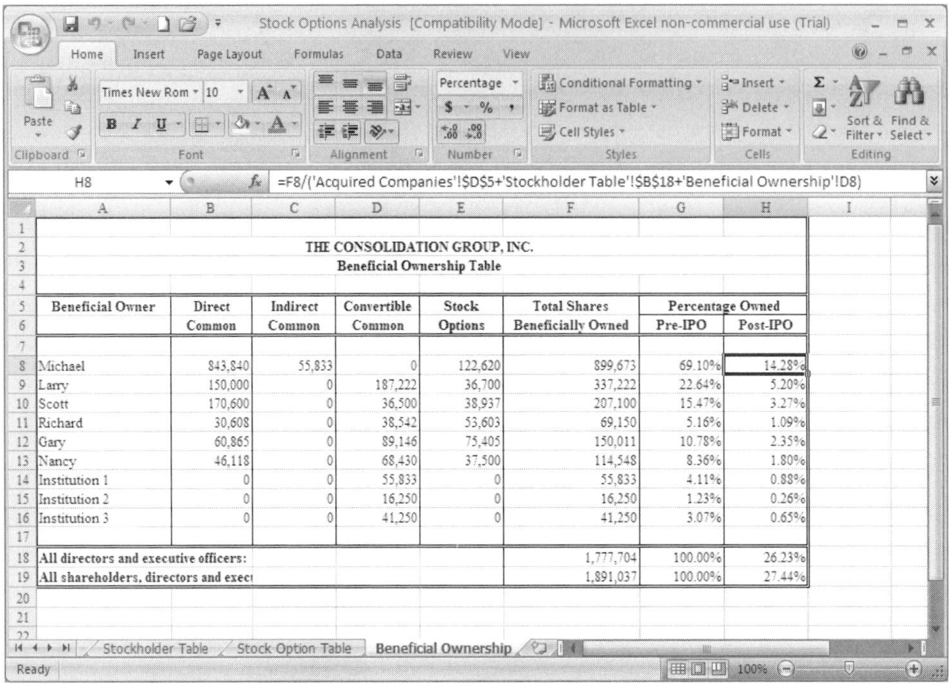

THE CONSOLIDATION GROUP, INC.
Beneficial Ownership Table

Beneficial Owner	Direct Common	Indirect Common	Convertible Common	Stock Options	Total Shares Beneficially Owned	Percentage Owned Pre-IPO	Percentage Owned Post-IPO
Michael	843,840	55,833	0	122,620	899,673	69.10%	14.28%
Larry	150,000	0	187,222	36,700	337,222	22.64%	5.20%
Scott	170,600	0	36,500	38,937	207,100	15.47%	3.27%
Richard	30,608	0	38,542	53,603	69,150	5.16%	1.09%
Gary	60,865	0	89,146	75,405	150,011	10.78%	2.35%
Nancy	46,118	0	68,430	37,500	114,548	8.36%	1.80%
Institution 1	0	0	55,833	0	55,833	4.11%	0.88%
Institution 2	0	0	16,250	0	16,250	1.23%	0.26%
Institution 3	0	0	41,250	0	41,250	3.07%	0.65%
All directors and executive officers:					1,777,704	100.00%	26.23%
All shareholders, directors and exec					1,891,037	100.00%	27.44%

Figure 5-23: Determining Shareholdings After the IPO

In showing you these business examples, my point is not to get caught up in complex math formulas. Rather, I want to emphasize how useful these simple, and sometimes not so simple, spreadsheets can be. When you are at the printer at 3:00 AM and someone announces that the sale price has dropped to $6 a share or that the offering has dropped from 3 million to 1.5 million shares, what do you do? Pull out a calculator or your pencil and trusty yellow pad? Maybe, but clearly there is a better way.

If you can create spreadsheets like these, you can react quicker to last-minute changes and be more accurate in your response. It matters not whether you create the initial sheets or have an accountant do it for you. Once you understand how they work, you have the tools you need to deal with the unexpected. And, you never know. It might get you home a little earlier. That, in itself, is not too bad.

Sorting and Filtering Your Data

You now know that Excel is a handy tool for working with numbers. I want to show you another facet of Excel, how it can be just as useful as a database. In this lesson, I will focus on using Excel to sort and filter data.

The Case of the Not-so Buggy Software

My software developer client was sued by its customer for buggy software. The customer manufactured snowboards (not really) and had paid $1.5 million for new three-tiered client server software to manage its manufacturing process. At the time, three-tiered client server products were a new phenomenon and all the rage in computer systems circles.

The installation process for this project was scheduled to take six months. (Heavy customization was required.) When the project went beyond deadline, the manufacturer got upset. After six more months passed with no success, the customer threw our people off the premises. The lawsuit followed on their heels.

The essence of the case was that the manufacturer had logged more than 140 bugs during the course of the failed installation. Brandishing a "bug log," which seemed several inches thick, opposing counsel pronounced the case a "slam dunk."

I came into the case toward the end of discovery. I can probably tell you now that my colleagues were not happy with our

71

position. One hundred forty-three seemed like a lot of bugs. The bug log, a long table with columns for date opened, date closed, description, comments, etc., seemed thicker than a phone book. They were heading for the bunker.

I concluded that the only hope of salvaging this case was to take control of the data—the bug log itself. The paper bug log was all but useless. There were so many bugs over so many pages that there was no hope of making sense out of it. So, I handed it to word processing and asked them to key it into an Excel spreadsheet.

After I added a few formatting touches, all of which you learned earlier, it looked something like this:

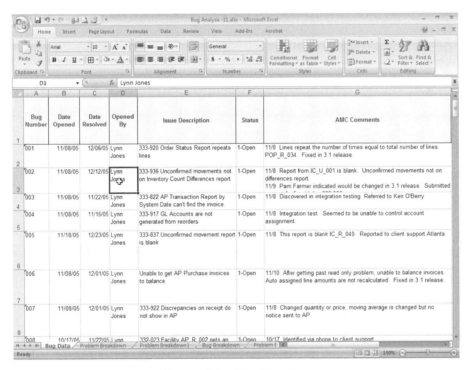

Figure 6-1: The Bug Log

Once we had the manufacturer's data in spreadsheet form, I began looking for ways to make sense of it. Since we had the "Date Opened" and "Date Resolved" data, one of my first steps was to add a column called "Days to Resolve."

Adding a column is easy. Right click on the column heading to the right of where you want to add the new column. Choose Insert. Excel adds a new column D and moves the information in the old column D to the right as column E. (All information to the right of old column D is moved one column to the right as well.) Then add a heading and formatting as appropriate.

Once I created the new column, it was simple to program Excel to calculate the number of days it took to resolve each bug. The formula is simply D2=C2-B2, D3=C3-B3, D4=C4-B4 and so on down the column.

Sidebar: Another Gotcha: Number Formatting Is Important

When I first applied the "Days to Resolve" formula, Excel presented me with a nonsensical date in response: 01/28/05. This stumped me for a minute until I checked the cell formatting and found that Excel had formulated the result as a date rather than a number. When I changed the formatting to a number, it produced the correct result: 28, which is the number of days difference between November 8, 2005 and December 6, 2005.

With more than 140 bugs at issue, it makes a difference whether you use the slow or the fast method of copying cell formulas. It could take 20 minutes to type in each formula:=C2-B2, =C3-B3, =C4-B4, etc. It could take five minutes just to cut and past the formula in each cell: Ctrl+C (copy) and Ctr+V 140 times (to paste it into each cell). You can achieve the same result in about 15 seconds by dragging the grab box for cell D2 down to cell D145 (the bottom of my spreadsheet). Watch as Excel scrolls downward for you as you hold the mouse at the bottom of the screen.

Here is the result:

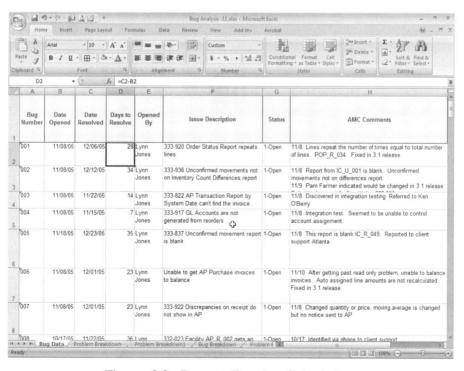

Figure 6-2: Days to Resolve Calculation

The next step was to try and better understand the nature of each complaint. In meeting with my client, I learned that some of the complaints were not bugs at all. Rather, the manufacturer had experienced setup problems, conflicts with other software, or had made an enhancement request. Since not all of the complaints were bugs, we needed a way to determine how many of each we were dealing with.

It was simple to add a new column called "Bug?". From there, we needed our client to analyze the complaints and grade them. I emailed the spreadsheet to my client and asked him to fill in the missing information, taking care to give the benefit of the doubt to the manufacturer.

By return email, I received a completed spreadsheet. Now I had the tools to begin my analysis.

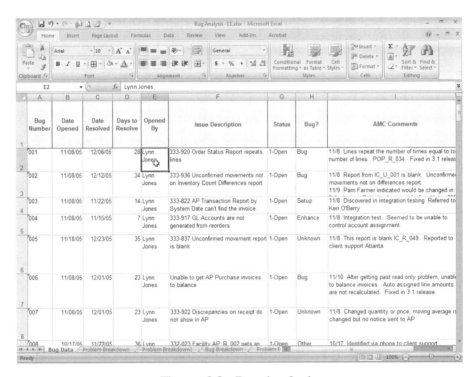

Figure 6-3: Bug Analysis

Sorting Data

There were two issues I wanted to track with this spreadsheet. First, I wanted to get an idea of how many bugs there were, versus how many other problems. Second, I wanted to get a better idea of how long it took to respond to problems.

One approach is to sort your data. Click on one of the cells in column D, say cell D3. You can sort all of the spreadsheet entries in ascending or descending order by clicking on the A-Z or Z-A Sort buttons. Since I wanted to see the worse case, I chose Z-A. Excel displayed the entries, which took the longest to resolve. Here is the result:

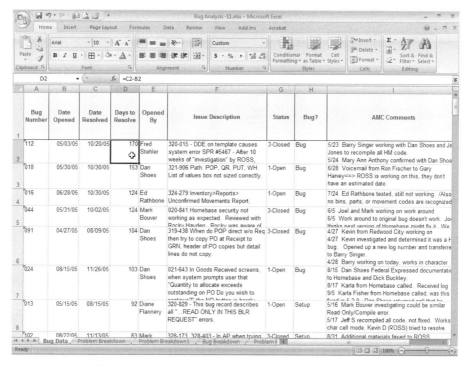

Figure 6-4: Reverse Sort of Days to Resolve

Just as quickly, you can sort the column in ascending order. Here are the results after clicking on the A-Z button:

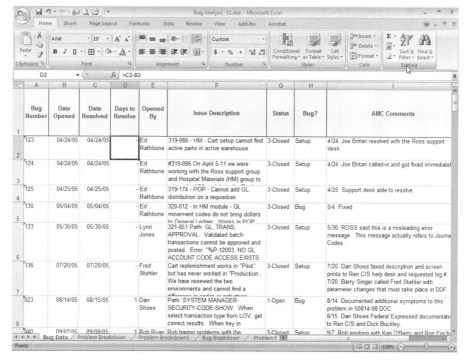

Figure 6-5: Ascending Sort of Days to Resolve

The same technique works for sorting column H, the "Bug?" column. You can sort the data alphabetically or in reverse alphabetical order. Try it for yourself.

A Trick for Viewing Your Data—Freezing the Panes

As you scroll down a long spreadsheet, you may find that you forget which column is which. One simple trick is to freeze a portion of the window. This allows the column headings to remain visible.

To accomplish this, click on the cell just below and to the right of the part of the portion of the screen you want to preserve. In this example, click on cell B2. Then choose the Freeze Panes option under the View menu, which you will find in the Window section of the Ribbon. It gives you the option to freeze the top row, to freeze the first column, or to freeze the section of the spreadsheet to the left and above the cell you are in. In this case, Column A and row 1, which are to the left and above cell B2, are frozen.

Scroll down your spreadsheet. Notice that the headings remain in view. Scroll to the right of your spreadsheet. Notice that the bug number in column A remains visible.

It looks like this:

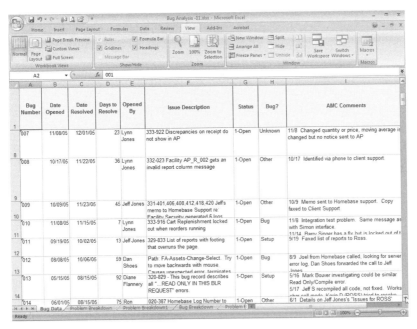

Figure 6-6: Freezing the Panes

One More Sorting Trick: Returning to Your Original Order

Once you sort your spreadsheet, there is no easy way to return it to its original order. For that reason, accountants long ago learned to add a column to their spreadsheet with sequential numbers—1-145, for example. They do this before sorting their data, so they can return the spreadsheet to its original order.

Creating the column and numbering it consecutively is rather simple. You create the column by right clicking on the column header (at the top) to the right of where you want it (column A for example) and choosing Insert. You can number the column consecutively by starting a list of numbers in, say, the first three cells and then highlighting them and dragging the grab bar down as far as you need to go. Excel automatically creates a series of numbers following the pattern you have started. We learned about this in Lesson 2.

Once you have the list, you can return your spreadsheet to its original order by clicking on your consecutively numbered column (column A, for example) and sorting it in ascending order. Voila, the spreadsheet is returned to its original order.

In this case, I had a column for bug numbers that was in consecutive order. Thus, to return my sheet back to its original order, I just sorted by that column.

Another Gotcha: Sorting the Column Header

When you sort your data, do not click on a column header to select your column. If you do, and then select the sort button, you may be sorry. Excel sorts only the figures in that column, leaving all of the other columns in their original state. This may render your data meaningless.

Let me make this clear with an example. If we want to sort our data by the type of bug, we can accomplish this by clicking on cell H2 and then choosing a Sort command. The entire spreadsheet is sorted per your command.

If, instead, we click on column heading H and then execute the Sort command, only that column is sorted. Bug number 123, which was a "setup" problem, would now be labeled as a true bug! This would be erroneous data and you would have big trouble.

Excel now gives you a warning if you try to sort this way and offers to expand your selection to the entire worksheet, something it didn't do in earlier versions of the program. All I can say is that I do not know why Excel included this feature, but watch out for it.

Advanced Sorting

Excel offers advanced sorting features, which go beyond the simple A-Z and Z-A buttons I showed you. Click on the Data option on the menu bar, select Sort, and you are presented with this screen.

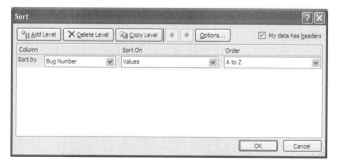

Figure 6-7: The Advanced Sort Box

For the most part, the options are self-explanatory, and you may not have many demands for the kind of multi-level sorting Excel provides. Nonetheless, it helps to be aware of these more advanced features. Check them out.

Filtering Your Data

Another way to get at your data is to filter it. Let's say we want to know how many bugs there really are, leaving out setup problems or enhancements. The approach we took earlier was to sort the data by the "Bug?" column and then scroll to the information we wanted to see. Now I want to show you how to filter your data so the bug information is all you see.

First, we put our spreadsheet back in its original order by sorting on column A, which is called "Bug Number." Our spreadsheet now looks like this:

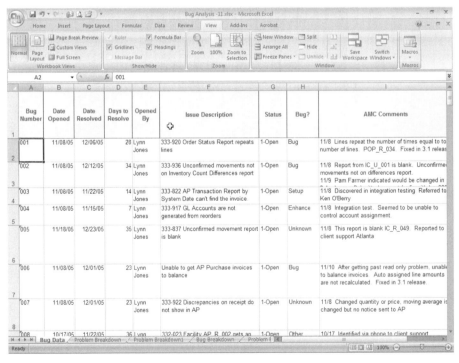

Figure 6-8: Filtering Data

Now, let's filter our data to show only the true bugs. Click on any cell in your spreadsheet. Then choose the Filter option under the Sort and Filter section of the Data menu. There is also an option for Advanced Filtering, which we can look at later. Your screen should look like this:

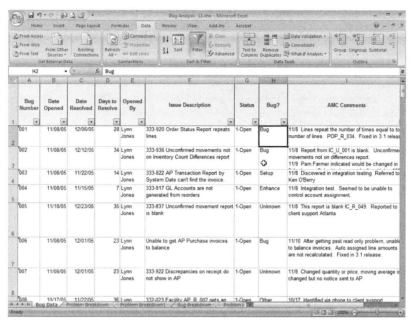

Figure 6-9: Auto Filtering

Notice the Down arrow buttons on each column heading. Excel automatically recognizes that your top row contains column headings. It uses them for your filtering commands.

Click on the arrow for the "Bug?" column. A drop-down list appears showing all of the items in that column: Bug, Dupe, Enhance, Other, Setup, Unknown. Like this:

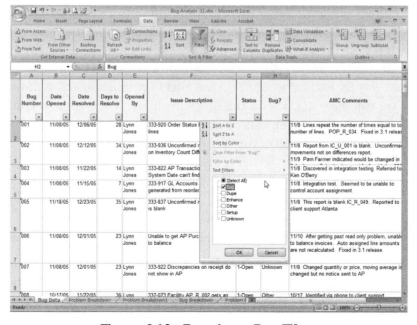

Figure 6-10: Running a Bug Filter

Choose "Bug" and your spreadsheet filters out all of the other categories. Now, only the data relating to bugs appears. Your sheet should look like this:

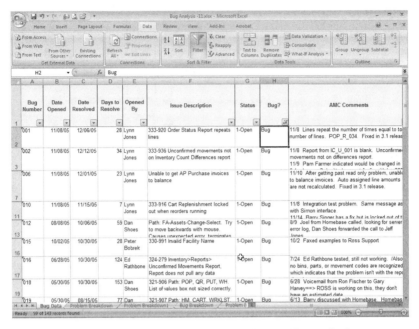

Figure 6-11: The Completed Filter—Bugs Only

Once you have filtered your data, there are lots of options available to you for analysis. You can sort the filtered data in any way you want. You can chart the data, as I will show you in the next lesson. Or, you can simply read through the data and see what you learn.

The point of filtering is noise/clutter reduction. When you are trying to analyze data, the first step is to clear away irrelevant information.

Let's try one more example to confirm how helpful filtering can be. Suppose we suspected that a substantial number of bugs had been logged by one individual, say Ed Rathbone. Rather than sort our data and scroll down to his entries, we can filter it. Click on the drop-down arrow for Column E and note that all of the people making entries are listed. Choose "Ed Rathbone" and notice how quickly you see all of the bugs he logged.

From there, you can analyze his bugs to see if any sort of pattern emerges. To remove the filter, click the same drop-down box and choose "All."

Advanced Filtering

Upon clicking the filter tabs, the third filtering option in Excel's drop-down filter list is a nested menu called Text Filters. Opening this menu gives you many options. Selecting Equals gives you a box like this:

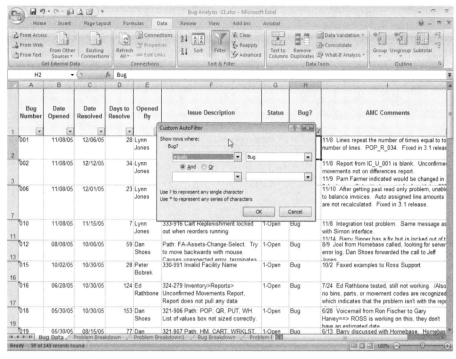

Figure 6-12: Custom AutoFilter Box

This box is pretty self-explanatory, but it adds power to your database filtering. It allows us, for example, to filter out all records except those initiated by Ed Rathbone or Diane Flannery.

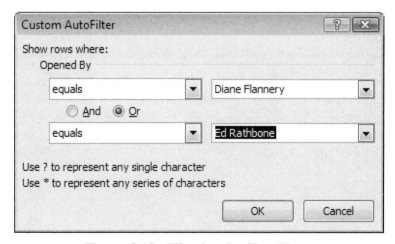

Figure 6-13: Filtering for Two Names

Our results look like this:

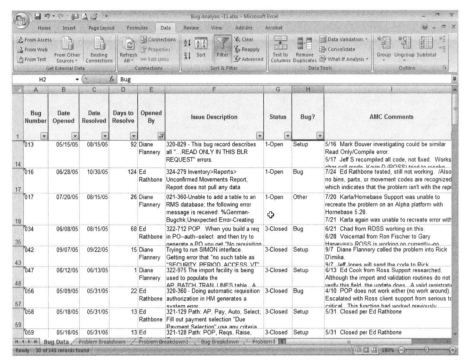

Figure 6-14: The Filtered Results

You will not need this kind of analytical power in all your cases, but it is nice to know it is there. Sorting and filtering data is simple with Excel and it might save you the trouble of setting up a database. It also might help your client avoid a trial.

Epitaph

Once we created a spreadsheet for the bug log, the data seemed to unlock. We learned that only a fraction of the problems were truly bugs and even fewer were critical bugs. While some problems took a long time to resolve, most were resolved within a few days. Suddenly, the case did not look as bad as it had. We had something to work with.

Charting Your Results

While many people realize that spreadsheets are handy for calculations, few know about their graphing and charting capabilities. That is a shame. The main reason I learned to use spreadsheets was to create visual exhibits for my cases. I did not realize how easy the formulas were until later.

In this lesson, I cover the basics of graphing and charting in Excel. As you will see, Excel makes it easy to create professional looking graphs and charts. Once you learn how, you will find reasons to use them in almost every type of communication, from trials and presentations to letters, briefs, and articles. The pictures you create will be worth a thousand words or more.

The Not-so Buggy Software Case Revisited

In the last lesson, we worked hard at analyzing a bug log prepared by my opponent in the case of the Not-so Buggy Software. We concluded that of the 140 plus bugs on the log, many were not bugs at all. In fact, only fifty-nine problems could fairly be called bugs. Of those bugs, only twenty-four were critical.

With numbers as simple and compelling as these, we could rest easy. But let's not stop there. Using Excel, we can create a visual representation, which will make the point even more strongly than the numbers themselves.

We start with a numerical breakdown of the bug log:

Breakdown of Bugs: Critical vs. Non-Critical			
Type	**Number**		
Critical	24		
Non-Critical	35		
Other Problems	85		
	144		

Figure 7-1: Bug Breakdown

Now let's create a chart to show this data. The first step is to highlight the cells in your spreadsheet containing the data being charted. Then highlight the labels for that data. In our case, the data is found in cells C5 through C7. The labels for that data are found in the adjoining cells, B5 through B7.

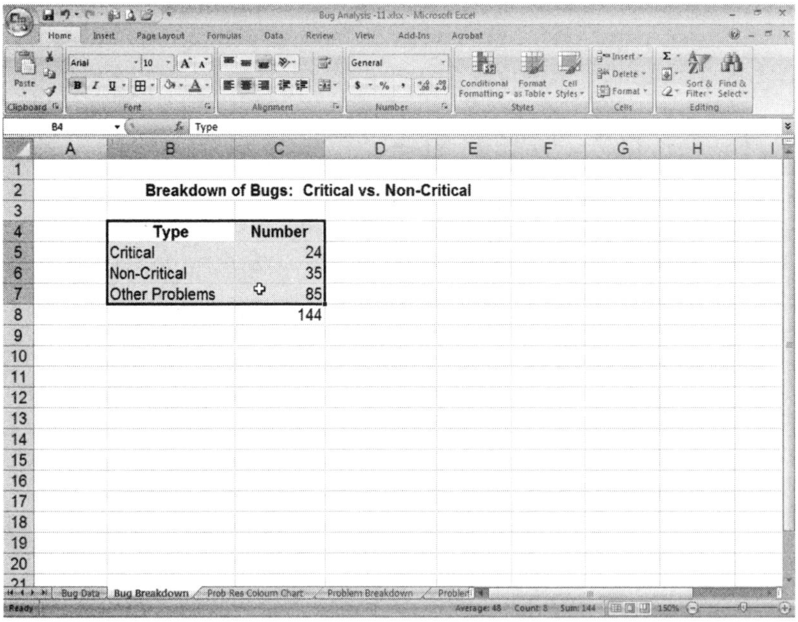

Figure 7-2: Charting the Data

Using the Charting Features

Once you have the data highlighted, choose the Insert menu and choose from the chart options. You can either pick a chart type directly or view all the chart options by clicking on the little arrow at the right side of the Chart menu.

The first step is to select the type of chart to use. There are various possibilities to be considered including a column chart, a line chart, a bar chart and a pie chart. There are other options as well but they don't apply to this exercise.

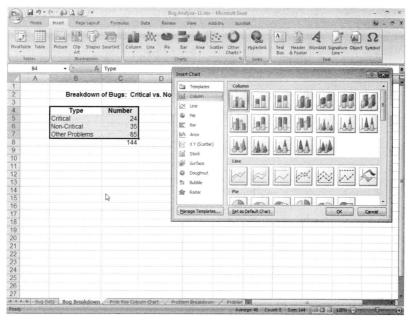

Figure 7-3: Viewing Chart Options

I suggest that we try a pie chart for this data. Notice that when you click on the Pie option, you have several Chart subtypes. I prefer the Pie with 3-D visual effects for our chart. It is the second option for Pie charts.

Once you are satisfied with the chart type, click OK at the bottom of the screen, which brings up a basic pie chart based on what you selected:

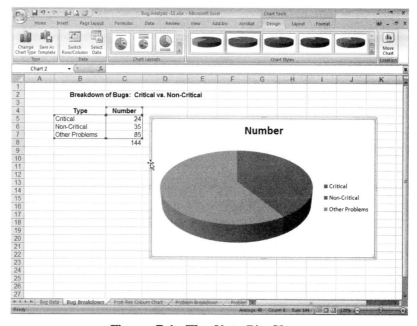

Figure 7-4: The New Pie Chart

Notice that a new menu item appears on your page called "Chart Tools." Beneath it are three new tabs that will appear any time you click on a chart. Explore each of these to get an idea of the options you have to format and work with your chart. I won't try and walk through all of the options Excel presents as they can be dizzying. I suggest you create a chart or two and play around with them yourself. Just see what happens, what you like and don't like.

The Select Data option under the Design menu can be important to you as you create more complex charts or want to change the underlying data in a chart. Click on it and you will see options to change the range of cells being referenced or to change the name of Chart labels and axis labels.

If you click on it, you will see a Select Data Source window that looks like this:

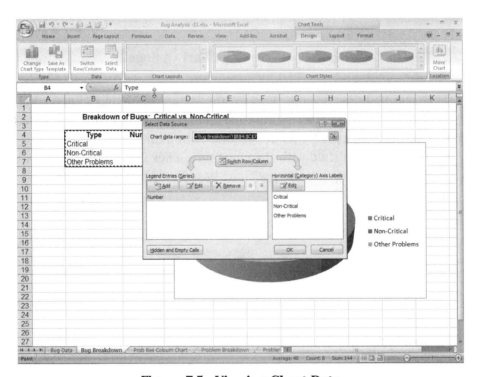

Figure 7-5: Viewing Chart Data

Click on Edit either to change the title for your Legend or to change the values that are being charted. In this case, we have the right data for our chart so we don't need to use this feature.

You also have the option to determine where you want to place your chart. This option is located on the right side of the Design menu under Move Chart Location. Click on the Move Chart and you will see something like the following:

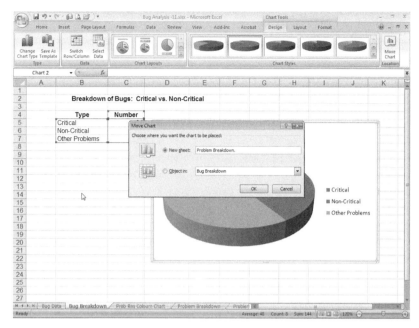

Figure 7-6: Move Chart Options

You can leave the chart on your existing spreadsheet or place it on a separate page. I like the latter option because I find it easier to work with charts that are a full page in size. Choose whichever option works best for you.

If you move your chart to a separate page, you should see something like this. (If not, do not worry because we will work through changing all the elements so you can make your chart look any way you want.)

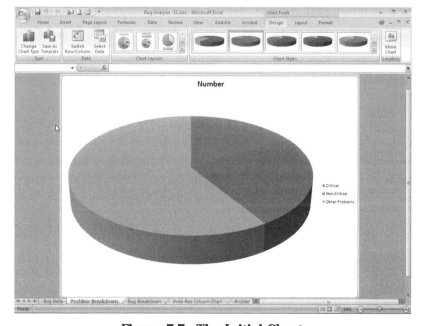

Figure 7-7: The Initial Chart

Formatting Your Chart

You can change just about every aspect of your chart from your chart worksheet, much of it by using the right mouse-click feature. Let's start with the title. Click in the title to change the text, let's change it to "Problem Breakdown." We can change the font size and color by right clicking and using the Format box options that appear.

Change the text color to dark blue and the font size to 28. The chart now looks like this:

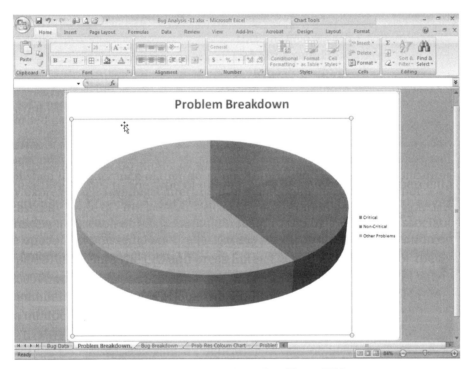

Figure 7-8: Changing the Chart Title

You can move your title anywhere on the chart you like. Select and grab it by holding down on the left mouse button and move it. Experiment with this standard Excel window feature until you feel comfortable with it. Or, get someone with more Excel experience to show you how to move, resize, and/or edit the title.

Let's edit the legend to our chart and the values for each section. Right click on the existing legend and a variety of options appear.

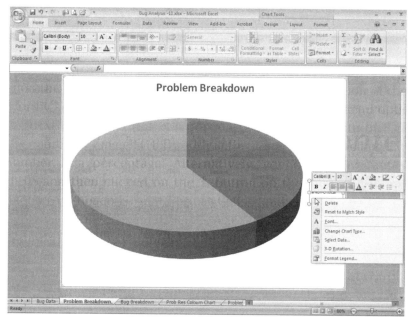

Figure 7-9: Legend Options Menu

From here, you can change the chart type, add or change source data, move the chart to a new location, or format the entire chart. Let's choose Format Legend and adjust the legend to our chart.

Figure 7-10: Formatting a Legend

Excel offers a number of places to place your legend, including top, bottom, right, or left. I chose right, in this case, but we need not stop there. You can move the legend anywhere you like by grabbing it (click on it and hold down the left mouse button) and moving it. You can also resize the legend box by grabbing any of the eight handles on its perimeter. And, you can enlarge or change the font used in the legend by right clicking on it and choosing Format Legend. (Actually there are several ways to change the legend format but this is as good a way as any.)

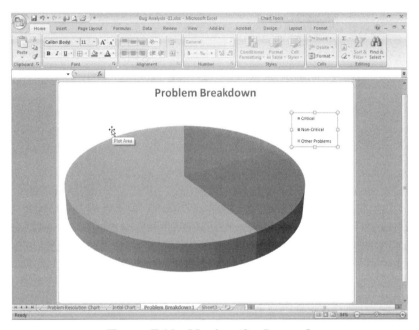

Figure 7-11: Moving the Legend

Our next step is to add labels to our pie slices to indicate the number of issues associated with each. Right click on any of the pie slices and choose the option to "Add Data Labels." The resulting numbers are pretty small but we can change the color, size and font easily by right clicking on any of them and then choosing from the different options.

We can move the numbers one at a time by clicking on each a second time. Notice that now only the selected label is highlighted. This means you have selected that one element. Formatting changes only affect that element and you can move or resize it separately from the other labels.

The same thing happens when you select pie elements (and later when you create other types of charts). If you click on a pie section, notice that all of the pieces are highlighted (small squares appear, one for each slice). Click a second time, and only that slice is selected. Through this mechanism, Excel allows you to format all of the slices at one time or each slice separately.

Let's go back to formatting our labels. Right click on any label and choose Format Data Labels. Let's make our labels bold white and 18 points in size. See the chart on the following page.

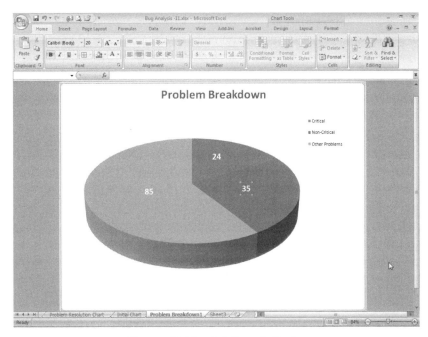

Figure 7-12: Adding Labels

We can enlarge the pie or move it anywhere in our chart space by selecting and dragging it. Selecting it is a bit counter-intuitive. Rather than click
on the pie itself, imagine a rectangle around the pie with borders outside the
pie at the top, bottom, right, and left. Click outside the pie but within the rectangle and a square box appears. Like this:

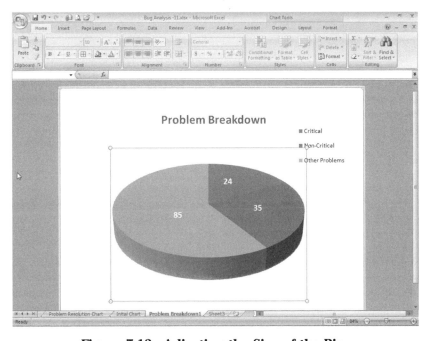

Figure 7-13: Adjusting the Size of the Pie

Grab one of the edges of the box and drag it wherever you like. Or, grab a corner and drag it to enlarge the pie. Feel free to move the legend or the title to a convenient location as well. The results might look like this:

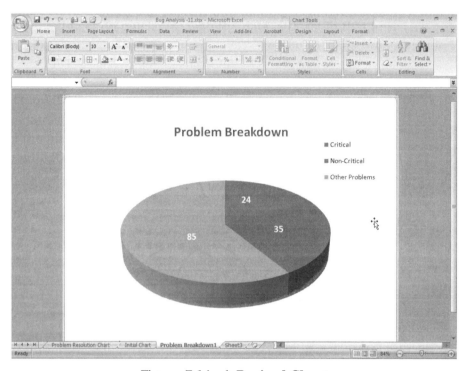

Figure 7-14: A Revised Chart

Now let's work on the pie itself. Right click on any slice and choose Format Data Series. The resulting menu (assuming you selected all the slices) allows you to rotate the pie, change the fill patterns, and/or change the data legends. Experiment with these options and see what happens. Note that a change in "area color" changes all the pie slices to that color (usually a bad idea).

After you exit from this menu, select a single pie slice (by clicking on it a second time). This time, you can act on the single slice. To change its fill color, for example, click on the Format option under Chart Tools and select Shape Fill from the Shape Styles section of the Ribbon. If you have only selected one section of the pie, this will allow you to change that color.

Once we have selected our slice colors, we may want to take one further formatting step. To emphasize how small the critical bug slice is, you can pull it away from the other slices of the pie. Do this by selecting that slice (by clicking a second time on the slice) and grabbing it. Pull it out from the pie slowly, and watch what happens. That slice becomes separated from the rest of the pie. See the chart on the following page.

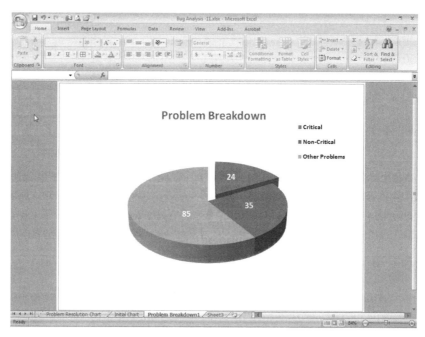

Figure 7-15: Pulling Out a Slice

There is a simple way to separate all the pieces of the pie at one time. Click once on the pie to select all the pieces. Then drag any slice out and watch as all three pieces separate.

As we move the pie pieces, we may need to move the data labels so they look right. We do this one label at a time, selecting and moving it where we want. Because the slices have different colors, we can also change the font colors for the individual labels. We do this by selecting each separately and formatting it using the right mouse click techniques I have already shown you.

Here is the final result. It is a good chart, suitable for presentation to the court, a client, or opposing counsel.

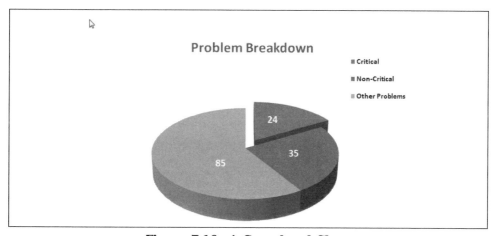

Figure 7-16: A Completed Chart

Annotating Your Chart

You can go further and add any kind of annotation to your chart. Suppose we wanted to further emphasize that the critical bugs were a small percentage of the whole. One approach is to add a text box and an arrow at the bottom of the chart. The text could say: "83% of the Problems Were Non-Critical!"

Annotation is relatively simple. Go to the Insert menu and choose the Text Box option. Then draw a text box at the bottom of your chart where you want the text to be (see Figure 7-17). Then type in the desired text and make formatting adjustments as needed.

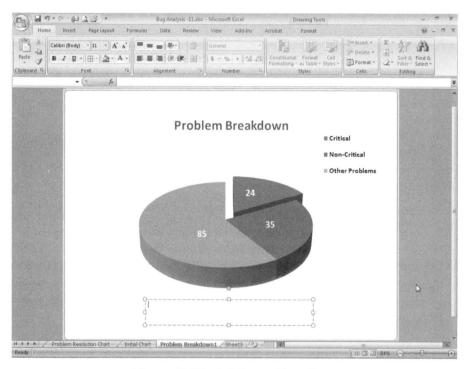

Figure 7-17: Adding a Text Box

Once you have entered your text, you have plenty of formatting options. Let's boldface the text and change the size to 16 points. Note that if your textbox is too small, you can grab one of the corner handles and expand it. You can move it by grabbing one of the sides of the textbox as well (Figure 7-18).

Once the text is properly formatted, you can add an arrow or other special effects to further make your point. (Actually, this might be overkill but I want to show you how to do it anyway.) Click on the Insert menu and go to Shapes under the Illustrations section. Choose an arrow or even a block arrow shape and then create it on your chart by clicking and dragging until you have the size and shape you need.

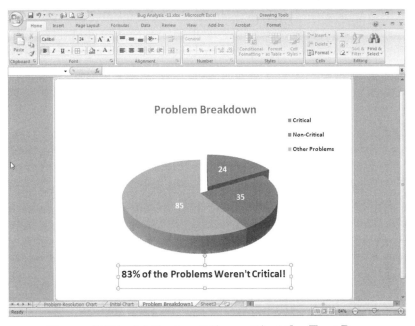

Figure 7-18: Adding and Formatting the Text Box

You can format the arrow in many ways. Notice that Drawing Tools appears as a new menu option. Click on the Format option under Drawing Tools and look at the different options available to you. You can choose different shapes, colors or styles for your arrow.

The resulting graphic may not be a work of art, but it does the job more effectively than numbers alone. And, it was relatively easy to create.

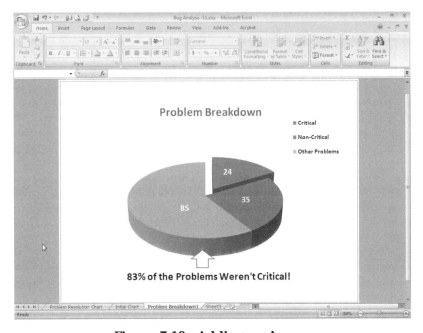

Figure 7-19: Adding an Arrow

For the artists out there, or even those with rudimentary graphics skills, I am not offering up this chart as a work of art. I just wanted to give you an idea of how easy it is to create a nice looking chart. From there, it is up to you. Practice your art and make it persuasive.

Creating Line Charts

One of the other issues we tracked in the bug case was our client's response time. Plaintiff claimed it took forever for my client to respond to problems. Lack of response time was so severe, it provided separate justification for the termination.

Taking data from our spreadsheet, we created a summary chart showing the number of problems opened each month and the number closed. The numbers did not seem to correspond with plaintiff's claim that my client totally ignored the problems raised.

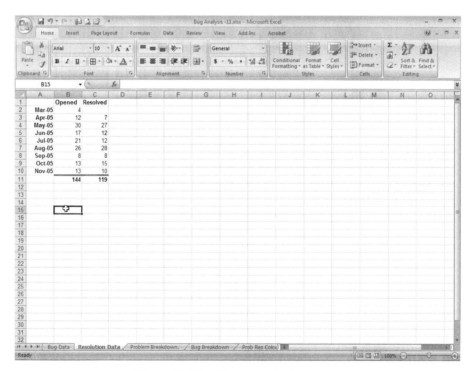

Figure 7-20: The Resolution Data

Once we had the numbers, the next step was to chart them. You already know something about the options available to you. This time we will choose a line chart. Chose the first line option and click OK. You will see your line chart on the worksheet page.

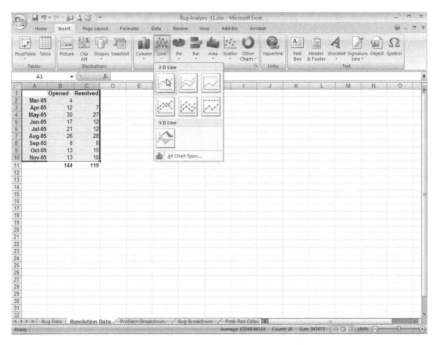

Figure 7-21: Creating a Line Chart

As you work through the Design menu, notice that you have two series of data. One series reflects the number of problems opened each month, and one reflects the number resolved.

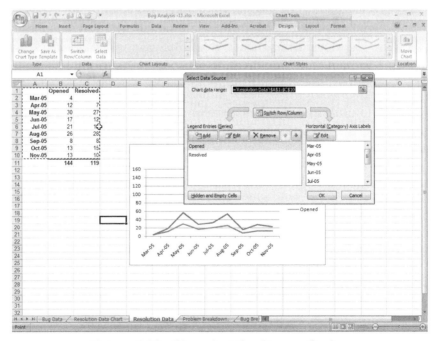

Figure 7-22: Choosing the Proper Series

After adding a title and placing the chart on a separate page in your workbook, we have something like this:

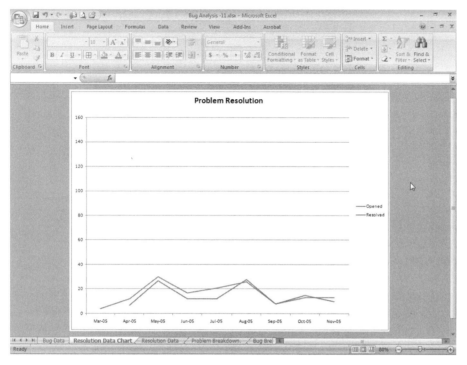

Figure 7-23: The Initial Chart

Now we have something to format. The first step is to change the scale of the Y axis. The range in my chart, from 0 to 160, is too great for my purposes. We do so by right clicking anywhere along the Y axis and choosing Format Axis. A familiar formatting box with a few different tabs appears. Choose Scale and change the maximum from 160 to something more appropriate, such as 35.

The next step is to change the line colors to make them more distinctive. Click on either line once, to select it, and then right click to bring up the Format Data Series menu. From there, it is a simple matter to choose your preferred color. Let's use red and blue for these lines.

It is likely that your background color differs from the yellow I am using. You can change background colors simply by right clicking anywhere in the field and choosing Format Plot Area. You can do the same thing for the entire chart by right clicking anywhere in the white space and choosing Format Chart Area.

The key here is that you can format/change any element in your chart by right clicking on it and following the menu instructions. There are too many options for me to cover, so I leave it to you to experiment. It will not take you long to gain an understanding of your options.

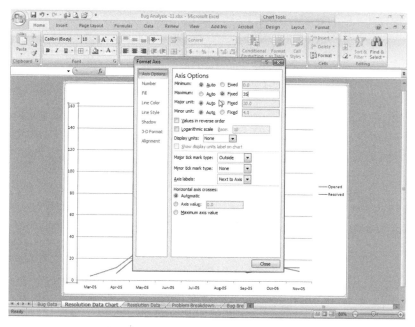

Figure 7-24: Formatting the Axis

My final steps in formatting this chart are to boldface and enlarge the title, boldface the Y and X axes, and add a legend. By now, you should know how to do this. You can bold both axes by clicking once in the chart area and then clicking on the B button in the toolbar (or use Ctrl+B). You can add the legend by right clicking on the chart area and choosing Chart Options. You already know how to reformat the title.

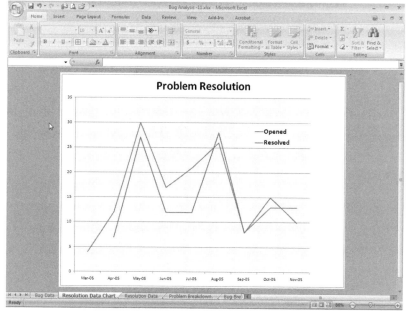

Figure 7-25: The Finished Chart

Making a Column Chart

Column charts are like line charts and just as simple to make. We could, for example, take the data used for our line chart and create the following column chart:

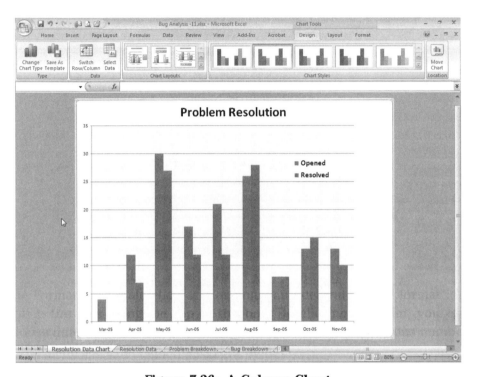

Figure 7-26: A Column Chart

You can reformat the chart in much the same fashion as we did for the line chart. Click on each series of columns to change their color. Right click in the white space to bring up the Chart Options menu to add a legend, boldface the chart, or add a title.

Mind you, a column chart doesn't make sense for this data but I wanted to show you how easy they are to create.

We have created several simple charts, which can be used to support almost any point. While Excel offers a number of different, fancier charts, I find that these are the ones I use. There is virtue in simplicity.

I do not want to close this lesson without making one last point. While Excel can help you create professional looking charts, it cannot tell you what to chart or, ultimately, how to make them persuasive. Determining what data needs to be charted, and how it will look are judgment calls that only you can make. My brief in this lesson is to show you what the possibilities are. Your job is to apply them to your situation.

Printing Your Work

Printing in Excel can be tricky. While word processing skills can get you part of the way, some printing techniques are unique to spreadsheets. In this last lesson, we will walk through the process for printing spreadsheets and charts. I will also show you how to insert a spreadsheet or chart into a word processing document or a PowerPoint slide.

Step One: What Do You Want to Print?

This is always the seminal question. If you want to print your entire spreadsheet, move to step two. If you do not, here is how Excel allows you to limit what you print.

We will return to our bug data file to work through these examples. You will recall that our spreadsheet looked like this:

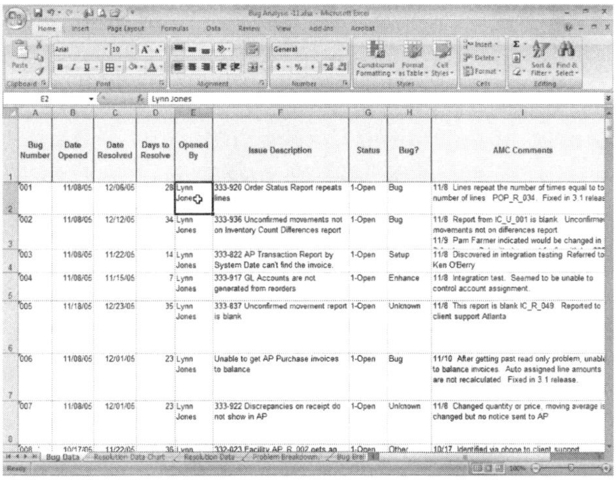

Figure 8-1: The Starting Spreadsheet

This spreadsheet extends for more than 140 rows and has 12 columns. Suppose we only want to print rows 1-5 and columns A-G? How do we limit our printing to those columns and rows?

Setting a Print Area

Excel solves this problem by allowing you to set a print area. In essence, you tell Excel how much of your spreadsheet you want to print.

Setting the print area is simple. Start by highlighting that portion of the spreadsheet you want to print. Then go to the Page Layout menu and select the Set Print Area option in the Page Setup section. Like this:

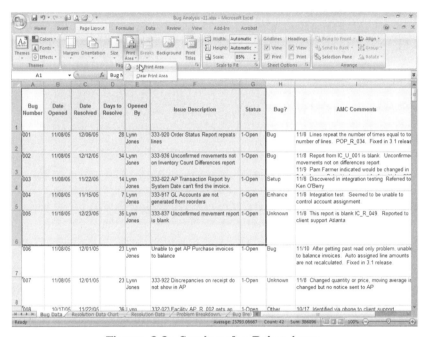

Figure 8-2: Setting the Print Area

Once you have set a print area, Excel honors your setting (and prints only the highlighted portion of your spreadsheet) until you clear the command. Choose the Clear Print Area option under the Set Print Area button. You do not have to clear the previous print area before you set a new one.

You can also set a print area in the Page Break Preview mode. To get there, click on the View menu and select Page Break Preview. This view is similar to the Normal view that we have been working with throughout this book. However, it also includes blue lines that show you how each spreadsheet page breaks. This is a handy feature, which we can discuss after I show you how to set a print area in the Page Break Preview mode.

To set a print area in the Page Break Preview mode, choose a print area just like we did in the Normal view. Then, instead of using the Set Print Area command from the Page Layout menu, simply right click on the highlighted area. One of the menu choices allows you to set your print area.

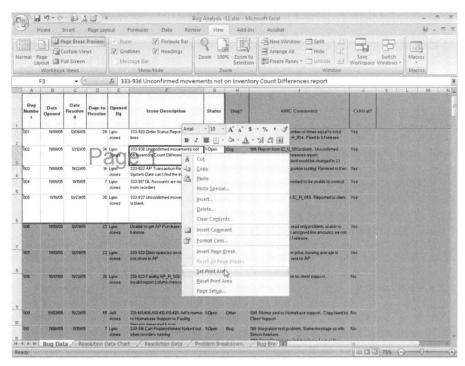

Figure 8-3: Another Way to Set a Print Area

Notice what happens when you set a limited print area. The rest of the spreadsheet turns gray. The gray area will not print.

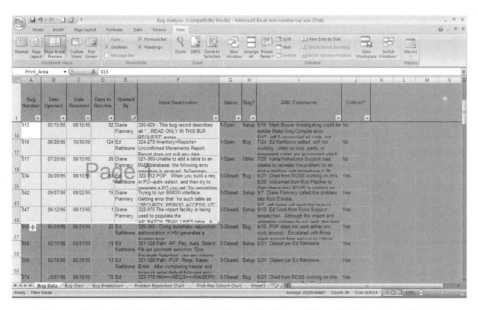

Figure 8-4: Setting the Print Area in Page Break Preview Mode

You can remove the print area in Page Break Preview mode. Just right click on any cell and choose Reset Print Area from the resulting menu.

Making Your Spreadsheet Fit on a Page

While we are still in Page Break Preview mode, let's address a slightly different problem. Suppose your spreadsheet is too wide to fit on a page or spills over onto the second page. How can you fit it on a single page?

With Page Break Preview, you can do this simply by dragging the blue lines to the appropriate column or row you want to fit on the page. For example, suppose we wanted to print rows 1 through 10 of our spreadsheet and columns A through I. We can limit our printing to that region by setting the print area. When we do this; however, we discover that it spills onto multiple pages as you can see below.

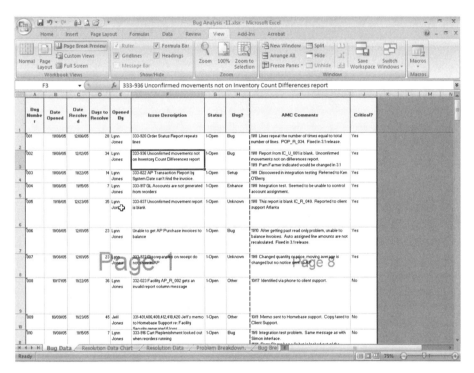

Figure 8-5: The Page Break Grid Lines

The solid blue lines show the portion of the spreadsheet that will print. The dashed lines show us where the pages break with our current printer settings.[2]

To make more of your spreadsheet print on a page, grab one or both dashed lines and drag them to the desired break point. For example, grab the dashed line to the right of column H and drag it to the right of column I. Grab

---

[2]You may have learned in working with your word processor that page breaks change depending on which printer you are using. That is true with spreadsheets as well. Before adjusting page breaks, make sure you have selected the printer you plan to use.

the dashed line below row 10 down to the bottom of row 11. Voila! Excel squeezes the print area you selected so it fits onto one page. The results look like this:

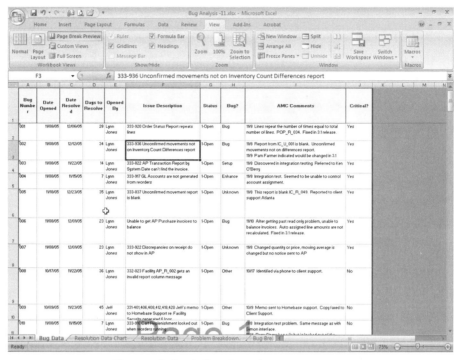

Figure 8-6: Adjusting the Page Break

What you have done is reduce the print size so that it fits the page. In the past, you had to experiment with reduced font sizes until you made the spreadsheet fit on the page. (And, you were stuck with the resulting reduced font size in your workbook until you changed it back.) Excel's Page Break Preview mode removes the difficulty. Sizing your print area to fit the page is simple and it does not affect the normal view of your workbook.

Step Two: Page Setup

Once you have set your print area and sized your spreadsheet to fit on one or more pages, the next step is to work through the Page Setup options. You can get there by clicking on the Office button and choosing Print Preview under the Print option.

I like Excel's Print Preview option because it allows me to see my document in a print preview mode and, also, it places most of the Page Setup and other printing options at my fingertips. See figure on next page.

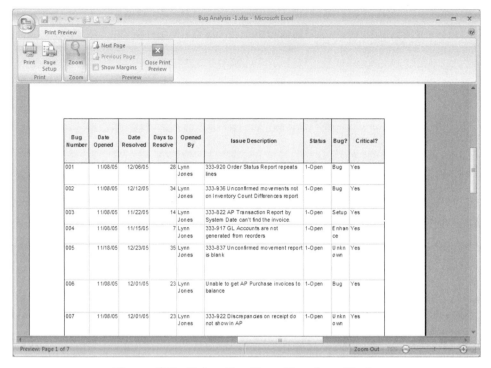

Figure 8-7: Using the Page Preview Mode

Headers and Footers

Click on the Page Setup button to create or adjust headers and footers. Excel brings up a tabbed Page Setup box, which controls headers and footers, margins, page choices, and sheet choices. Let's start with Header and Footer commands.

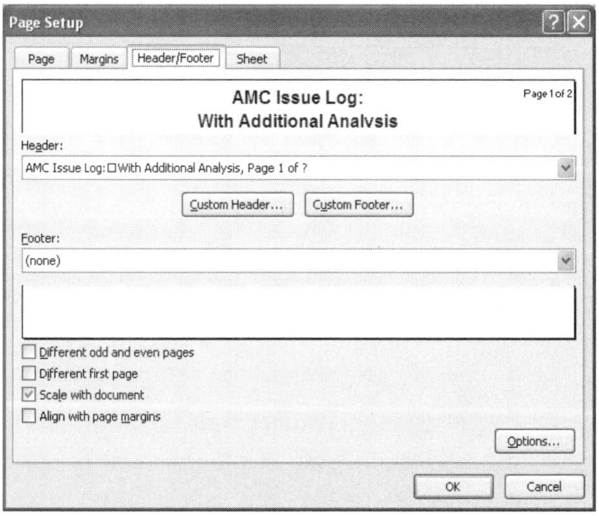

Figure 8-8: The Page Setup Box

The Page Header appears at the top of each spreadsheet page. Excel provides a number of standard headers, which you can access by clicking on the Down arrow to the right of the Header box. Try a few of these and see what happens.

You can create a custom header by clicking on the Custom Header button. When you do, Excel presents you with this box:

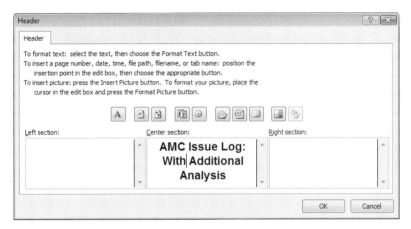

Figure 8-9: Setting a Custom Header

As you can see, the header is divided into three sections. You can use all or any one of them for your header. In this case, I have typed in a header myself. I have enlarged and boldfaced the font by blocking my text and clicking on the Font button (you can also make these settings before you type the text).

Excel allows a number of automatic header inserts as well. Click on the Page button and Excel automatically shows the page number. Click on the Pages button and Excel shows how many pages are in the sheet.

For example, if we want our header to state: Page ___ of ____. Use Excel's Page and Pages buttons to insert the header through a combination of typed words and Excel commands. The header looks like this:

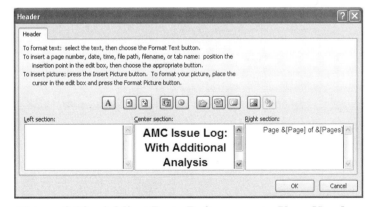

Figure 8-10: Adding Page References to Your Header

The resulting spreadsheet looks like this:

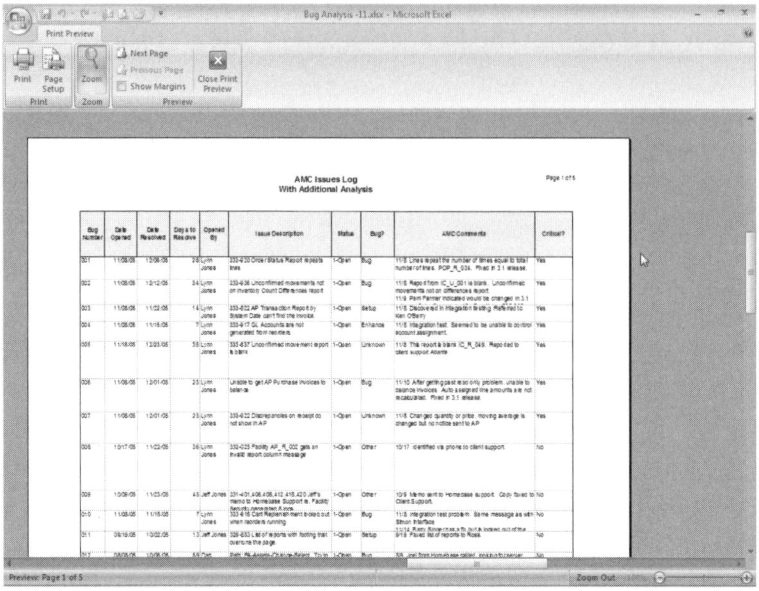

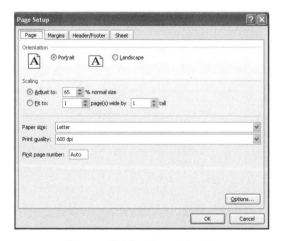

Figure 8-11: Previewing the Custom Header

Experiment with the rest of the buttons. You can insert a date, time, file-name, or the name of the particular spreadsheet you are printing.

Footers work just like headers. You can create a custom footer or use any of Excel's preset footers. The buttons work the same whether you are using them for headers or footers.

Page and Sheet Commands

Click on the Page tab in the Page Setup box. Choose here whether to print in portrait or landscape mode and the paper size. You can also tell Excel to print your spreadsheet in a certain number of pages or to reduce or enlarge its size to a certain percentage.

Figure 8-12: Page Options

Select the Sheet tab. From here, you can tell Excel to print grid lines (the default is to leave them out). You can also tell Excel to print row and column headings on each page and set an order for page printing.

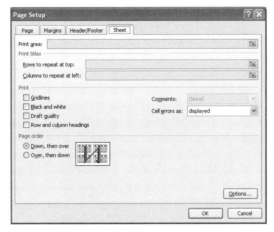

Figure 8-13: The Sheet Tab

You cannot access the print area and the rows and columns to repeat from the Print Preview mode. If you want to specify these options, exit the Print Preview mode and instead go to the Page Layout menu. From there click on the Print Titles button in the Page Setup Section. Then you will see the Page Setup window and it will let you select rows and columns that you may want to repeat on each printed page.

Margins

There are two ways to set margins, and both are accessible from the Print Preview mode. From the Page Setup box, choose the Margin tab. The following box allows you to enter numerical settings and is self-explanatory.

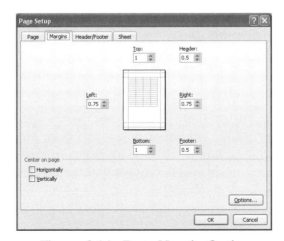

Figure 8-14: Page Margin Options

You can also set margins directly from the Print Preview mode. Click on the Margins button in Print Preview, and Excel displays lines showing all of the margins used.

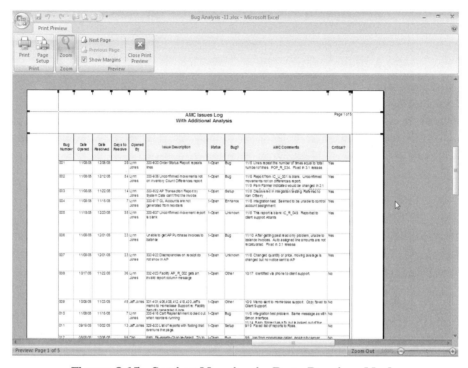

Figure 8-15: Setting Margins in Page Preview Mode

Any of these lines can be moved by dragging them. The only limits are those set by your printer, which typically requires a certain minimum margin around the page.

Step Three: Print Away

Once you have set your print area, adjusted your margins, and added headers and footers, you are ready to print. Click on the Print button, Ctrl+P, or choose Print from within the Office menu. Your choice.

Whichever way you get there, you will see Excel's Print box. The default is to print the spreadsheet on which you have been working—the active sheet. You can print all of it or select certain pages of it to print. As an alternative, you can select a range of cells and print only that selection. Or, you can print the entire workbook.

Figure 8-16: The Print Box

There is a simple trick for printing more than one spreadsheet—but not the entire workbook—at a time. In the normal spreadsheet view, select multiple spreadsheets by clicking on each tab and holding down the Shift key (for choosing consecutive spreadsheets) or the Ctrl key (to select non-consecutive spreadsheets). Once you have selected the sheets, execute the Print command. The print settings default to the Active sheet(s). When you command Excel to print, it prints all the selected spreadsheets.

Placing a Chart or Spreadsheet into Word or PowerPoint

Thus far, we have focused on printing our work as a stand-alone document. To close out this lesson, I want you to be aware of another option. Rather than printing your spreadsheet separately, you can integrate it into a word processing document or into a PowerPoint presentation. The combined results can be quite effective in getting your message across.

For these examples, I will focus on Microsoft's sister suite applications: Word and PowerPoint. If you use other products such as Corel's WordPerfect or Lotus' Word Pro, the same techniques should work, but you will have to try them for yourself. I use the Microsoft products and there are too many combinations of other products and possible program conflicts for me to test them all.

Word

Placing an Excel chart into a Word document is relatively simple. Start by clicking on the chart to select it. You can select a chart by clicking anywhere on the perimeter of the chart. Notice that a gray selection box appears around the perimeter of the chart.

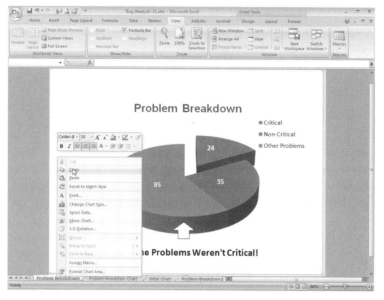

Figure 8-17: Copying a Chart from Excel

Once you have selected the chart, copy it using Ctrl+C or the Copy command on the Home menu.

Switch to Word and find the space where you want to place the chart. Paste it at that point using whichever paste method you prefer. You can paste it in normally or use the Paste Special option to insert it as a graphic or even a live spreadsheet. Your chart appears in your document at the selected location like this:

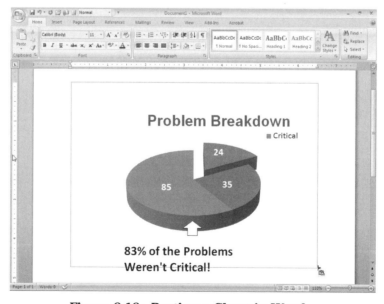

Figure 8-18: Pasting a Chart in Word

There are a number of word processing tricks you can use to better place your charts in the documents. You can add a frame and set the text attributes so that it flows around your chart. Regrettably, these features are beyond the scope of this book. I just want you to know how simple it is to integrate your Excel charts with your written work product.

Placing an Excel spreadsheet into Word is equally simple. Select the cells you want to use and copy them to the clipboard. Switch to Word and find the place where you want to add the spreadsheet. Paste the cells.

The trick is to use the Paste Special command rather than the Paste command. If you merely paste the spreadsheet cells, Word converts them into a table. If you execute the Paste Special command, and choose to paste the cells as an Excel Worksheet Object, Word treats the pasted cells as a spreadsheet. Double click on the object and it opens with Excel, giving you all of the original spreadsheet options for updating, editing, and formatting. Try adding a border or shading around the object as well. Here is how it might look:

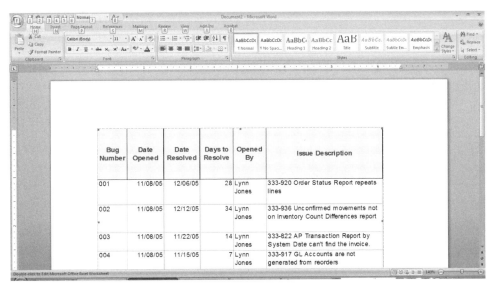

Figure 8-19: Pasting a Spreadsheet In Word

PowerPoint

Placing a chart in PowerPoint is as easy as placing it in Word. Copy the chart and paste it into a slide. Once it is there, you can size and move it using PowerPoint's standard Windows commands. To enlarge it, grab one of the sizing handles and drag the border to the desired height or width. Hold down the

Ctrl key as you size the image and it expands or contracts keeping its original proportions.

You can paste a spreadsheet into PowerPoint either as an Excel object (which is editable) or as an image. Use the normal Paste command to import it in as an image. Use the Paste Special command to keep it as an editable Excel worksheet.

Appendix

What's New in Excel 2007?

What's changed in Excel 2007 over earlier versions of the product? Not much, actually. Most of the important functionality has been in the product since at least Excel 97. You can make spreadsheets, use formulas, calculate values and create slick-looking charts, just like you could in all of the previous versions. To be sure, the new version allows you to go way beyond the 65,000 row limitation of past versions (and use more columns than I could ever imagine), but there aren't that many other substantive changes. You now have a few more color options for cells and the charts look a bit prettier, but that is about it. Certainly not much has changed that will likely affect your legal practice, or mine for that matter.

But at one level a lot has changed and I am not sure it is for the better. Office 2007 dramatically changed how programs like Excel look and work by tossing out the familiar menu-driven toolbars in favor of what they call the "Ribbon." The Ribbon takes up a lot of space at the top of your screen and is supposed to be more intuitive for new users. Here is how the Ribbon looks:

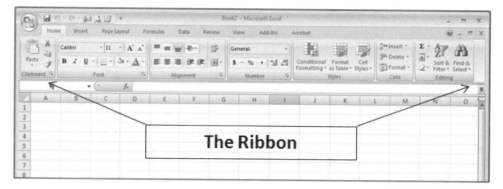

Appendix 1: Excel 2007's New Ribbon Feature

The Ribbon replaces the traditional menu options that used to appear when you clicked on one of the menu items, like File, Edit, View, etc. Instead, you have a different list of menu options to choose from and a very different display when you choose each. Thus, from the new "Home" menu, I see a series of what I call sections, but you could call them groups or sub-menus (or even toolbars) if you like. Thus, the Home menu has sections for the Clipboard, Font, Alignment, Number, Styles, etc. Other menu options have other groups.

There is also a new Office Button at the top left of the screen. This opens up something that looks more like a traditional menu and includes a number of important choices, including Open, Save, Print and a list of recently-opened documents. If you are used to using menu toolbars rather than hot keys to do things like open and save files, you will be clicking here a lot.

You can add some of your favorite items to a spot on top of the menu bar, which Microsoft calls the Quick Access Toolbar. You can see from the illustration that I added several, including Save, the Undo and Redo buttons, email, etc. Unfortunately, to my way of thinking, there are only a limited number of items that can be added. The rest you have to find on the Ribbon, if you can.

I hated the Ribbon when I first tried Excel 2007, back when it was in Beta. I had become quite proficient with the menu/toolbar approach of earlier versions and the Ribbon set me back quite a bit. "What happened to all of my toolbars?" I cried as I fumbled around looking for things. In many cases, I couldn't find what I was looking for and had to use the search feature in Help, which was moved as well to a little question mark on the right of the page.

Ultimately, I got used to most of the changes and I can find what I need with reasonable speed, although I still fumble a bit as I work on new projects. And, I have to admit, Microsoft got some things right in the new version. Sizing a spreadsheet used to require that I click a drop-down menu and choose from several preset sizes. With 2007, they added a little magnifying slider bar at the bottom right of the screen that I kind of like. The charts are prettier too, although they managed to mess up all the right click options that used to be so simple and straight forward. Why Microsoft would go to such trouble to mess up all the good things they create is simply beyond me.

But maybe I am just a Luddite. I understand Microsoft tested the new interface with thousands of users and claims it is easier to learn and master. Could be, but the jury is still out for me. Check back in a year or so for an update and we will see.

Don't let this Ribbon business get in the way of the main point here. Regardless of version, Excel is a powerful program that you should be using in your practice. It offers number and charting features that you can easily employ every day whether you are a litigator, business lawyer or any other member of the legal services team. Dig in, start clicking around and go wild. You will be finding new uses for these handy tools everywhere you go. I hope you find them as helpful as I do.

Index

The Lawyers Guide to Collaboration Tools and Technologies: Smart Ways to Work Together
By Dennis Kennedy and Tom Mighell

This first-of-its-kind guide for the legal profession shows you how to use standard technology you already have and the latest "Web 2.0" resources and other tech tools, like Google Docs, Microsoft Office and SharePoint, and Adobe® Acrobat, to work more effectively on projects with colleagues, clients, co-counsel and even opposing counsel. In *The Lawyer's Guide to Collaboration Tools and Technologies: Smart Ways to Work Together*, well-known legal technology authorities Dennis Kennedy and Tom Mighell provides a wealth of information useful to lawyers who are just beginning to try these tools, as well as tips and techniques for those lawyers with intermediate and advanced collaboration experience.

The Lawyer's Guide to Marketing on the Internet, Third Edition
By Gregory H. Siskind, Deborah McMurray, and Richard P. Klau

In today's competitive environment, it is critical to have a comprehensive online marketing strategy that uses all the tools possible to differentiate your firm and gain new clients. The Lawyer's Guide to Marketing on the Internet, in a completely updated and revised third edition, showcases practical online strategies and the latest innovations so that you can immediately participate in decisions about your firm's Web marketing effort. With advice that can be implemented by established and young practices alike, this comprehensive guide will be a crucial component to streamlining your marketing efforts.

The Lawyer's Field Guide to Effective Business Development
By William J. Flannery, Jr.

"In this wonderful book, Bill Flannery, who changed the legal marketplace forever, does what he's been doing so effectively throughout his extraordinary career—he teaches lawyers how to sell. How can you build your firm's business without it?"
— Richard S. Levick, Esq., President and CEO, Levick Strategic Communications

Long-term, profitable client relationships form the foundation for the enduring success of any law firm. Winning and retaining long-term, attractive clients doesn't happen by accident. In his new book, The Lawyer's Field Guide to Effective Business Development, renowned legal marketer Bill Flannery shares his practical approach to acquiring and refining the face-to-face skills necessary for winning and keeping valuable clients.

In a handy, pocket-sized format, this unique guidebook is designed so you can take it with you as you travel in search of new business. The chapters are organized chronologically to take you step by step from your initial search for clients through the process of building and maintaining long-term profitable client relationships.

The Electronic Evidence and Discovery Handbook: Forms, Checklists, and Guidelines
By Sharon D. Nelson, Bruce A. Olson, and John W. Simek

The use of electronic evidence has increased dramatically over the past few years, but many lawyers still struggle with the complexities of electronic discovery. This substantial book provides lawyers with the templates they need to frame their discovery requests and provides helpful advice on what they can subpoena. In addition to the ready-made forms, the authors also supply explanations to bring you up to speed on the electronic discovery field. The accompanying CD-ROM features over 70 forms, including, Motions for Protective Orders, Preservation and Spoliation Documents, Motions to Compel, Electronic Evidence Protocol Agreements, Requests for Production, Internet Services Agreements, and more. Also included is a full electronic evidence case digest with over 300 cases detailed!

The Lawyer's Guide to Adobe® Acrobat, Third Edition
By David L. Masters

This new edition was written to help lawyers increase productivity, decrease costs, and improve client services by moving from paper-based files to digital records. This updated and revised edition focuses on the ways lawyers can benefit from using the most current software, Adobe® Acrobat 8, to create Portable Document Format (PDF) files. The latest version of Acrobat has a number of useful features for the legal professional, including Bates numbering and redaction.

The Lawyer's Guide to Microsoft Outlook 2007
By Ben M. Schorr

Outlook is the most used application in Microsoft Office, but are you using it to your greatest advantage? The Lawyer's Guide to Microsoft Outlook 2007 is the only guide written specifically for lawyers to help you be more productive, more efficient and more successful. More than just email, Outlook is also a powerful task, contact, and scheduling manager that will improve your practice. From helping you log and track phone calls, meetings, and correspondence to archiving closed case material in one easy-to-store location, this book unlocks the secrets of "underappreciated" features that you will use every day. Written in plain language by a twenty-year veteran of law office technology and ABA member, you'll find:

- Tips and tricks to effectively transfer information between all components of the software
- The eight new features in Outlook 2007 that lawyers will love
- A tour of major product features and how lawyers can best use them
- Mistakes lawyers should avoid when using Outlook
- What to do when you're away from the office

The Lawyer's Guide to Marketing Your Practice, Second Edition

Edited by James A. Durham and Deborah McMurray
This book is packed with practical ideas, innovative strategies, useful checklists, and sample marketing and action plans to help you implement a successful, multi-faceted, and profit-enhancing marketing plan for your firm. Organized into four sections, this illuminating resource covers: Developing Your Approach; Enhancing Your Image; Implementing Marketing Strategies and Maintaining Your Program. Appendix materials include an instructive primer on market research to inform you on research methodologies that support the marketing of legal services. The accompanying CD-ROM contains a wealth of checklists, plans, and other sample reports, questionnaires, and templates—all designed to make implementing your marketing strategy as easy as possible!

The 2009 Solo and Small Firm Legal Technology Guide

By Sharon D. Nelson, John Simek, and Michael C. Maschke
This annual guide is the only one of its kind written to help solo and small firm lawyers find the best legal technology for their dollar. You'll find the most current information and recommendations on computers, servers, networking equipment, legal software, printers, security products, smartphones, and anything else a law office might need. It's written in plain language to make implementation easier if you choose to do it yourself—or you can use it in conjunction with your IT consultant. Either way, you'll learn how to make technology work for you.

The Lawyer's Guide to Strategic Planning: Defining, Setting, and Achieving Your Firm's Goals

By Thomas C. Grella and Michael L. Hudkins
This practice-building resource is your guide to planning dynamic strategic plans and implementing them at your firm. You'll learn about the actual planning process and how to establish goals in key planning areas such as law firm governance, competition, opening a new office, financial management, technology, marketing and competitive intelligence, client development and retention, and more. The accompanying CD-ROM contains a wealth of policies, statements, and other sample documents. If you're serious about improving the way your firm works, increasing productivity, making better decisions, and setting your firm on the right course, this book is the resource you need.

The Successful Lawyer: Powerful Strategies for Transforming Your Practice

By Gerald A. Riskin
Available as a Book, Audio-CD Set, or Combination Package.
Global management consultant and trusted advisor to many of the world's largest law firms, Gerry Riskin goes beyond simple concept or theory and delivers a book packed with practical advice that you can implement right away. By using the principles found in this book, you can live out your dreams, embrace success, and awaken your firm to its full potential. Large law firm or small, managing partners and associates in every area of practice—all can benefit from the information contained in this book. With this book, you can attract what you need and desire into your life, get more satisfaction from your practice and your clients, and do so in a systematic, achievable way.

How to Start and Build a Law Practice, Platinum Fifth Edition

By Jay G Foonberg
This classic ABA bestseller has been used by tens of thousands of lawyers as the comprehensive guide to planning, launching, and growing a successful practice. It's packed with over 600 pages of guidance on identifying the right location, finding clients, setting fees, managing your office, maintaining an ethical and responsible practice, maximizing available resources, upholding your standards, and much more. You'll find the information you need to successfully launch your practice, run it at maximum efficiency, and avoid potential pitfalls along the way. If you're committed to starting—and growing—your own practice, this one book will give you the expert advice you need to make it succeed for years to come.

Flying Solo: A Survival Guide for Solo and Small Firm Lawyers, Fourth Edition

Edited by K. William Gibson
This fourth edition of this comprehensive guide includes practical information gathered from a wide range of contributors, including successful solo practitioners, law firm consultants, state and local bar practice management advisors, and law school professors. This classic ABA book first walks you through a step-by-step analysis of the decision to start a solo practice, including choosing a practice focus. It then provides tools to help you with financial issues including banking and billing; operations issues such as staffing and office location and design decisions; technology for the small law office; and marketing and client relations. Whether you're thinking of going solo, new to the solo life, or a seasoned practitioner, *Flying Solo* provides time-tested answers to real-life questions.

LawPracticeManagementSection
MARKETING • MANAGEMENT • TECHNOLOGY • FINANCE

30-Day Risk-Free Order Form
Call Today! 1-800-285-2221
Monday–Friday, 7:30 AM – 5:30 PM, Central Time

Qty	Title	LPM Price	Regular Price	Total
_____	The Lawyer's Guide to Collaboration Tools and Technologies: Smart Ways to Work Together (5110589)	$59.95	$ 89.95	$_____
_____	The Lawyer's Guide to Marketing on the Internet, Third Edition (5110585)	74.95	84.95	$_____
_____	The Lawyer's Field Guide to Effective Business Development (5110578)	49.95	59.95	$_____
_____	The Electronic Evidence and Discovery Handbook: Forms, Checklists, and Guidelines (5110569)	99.95	129.95	$_____
_____	The Lawyer's Guide to Adobe® Acrobat, Third Edition (5110588)	49.95	79.95	$_____
_____	The Lawyer's Guide to Microsoft Outlook 2007 (5110661)	49.95	69.95	$_____
_____	Trainer's Manual for the Law Firm Associate's Guide to Personal Marketing and Selling Skills (5110581)	49.95	59.95	$_____
_____	The Lawyer's Guide to Marketing Your Practice, Second Edition (5110500)	79.95	89.95	$_____
_____	The 2009 Solo and Small Firm Legal Technology Guide (5110657P)	54.95	84.95	$_____
_____	The Lawyer's Guide to Strategic Planning (5110520)	59.95	79.95	$_____
_____	The Successful Lawyer: Powerful Strategies for Transforming Your Practice (5110531)	64.95	84.95	$_____
_____	How to Start and Build a Law Practice, Platinum Fifth Edition (5110508)	57.95	69.95	$_____
_____	Flying Solo: A Survival Guide for Solo and Small Firm Lawyers, Fourth Edition (5110527)	79.95	99.95	$_____

*Postage and Handling	
$10.00 to $24.99	$5.95
$25.00 to $49.99	$9.95
$50.00 to $99.99	$12.95
$100.00 to $349.99	$17.95
$350 to $499.99	$24.95

**Tax
DC residents add 5.75%
IL residents add 9.00%

*Postage and Handling	$_____
**Tax	$_____
TOTAL	$_____

PAYMENT

❏ Check enclosed (to the ABA)

❏ Visa ❏ MasterCard ❏ American Express

_____
Account Number   Exp. Date   Signature

Name _____ Firm _____

Address _____

City _____ State _____ Zip _____

Phone Number _____ E-Mail Address _____

Guarantee
If—for any reason—you are not satisfied with your purchase, you may return it within 30 days of receipt for a complete refund of the price of the book(s). No questions asked!

Mail: ABA Publication Orders, P.O. Box 10892, Chicago, Illinois 60610-0892
♦ **Phone: 1-800-285-2221** ♦ **FAX: 312-988-5568**

E-Mail: abasvcctr@abanet.org ♦ **Internet: http://www.lawpractice.org/publications**